inspired so many. For those who never met him, the book provides an authentic encounter with a true disciple of Christ. For us who did know him, it is a welcome but provisional reunion with a man who meant so much."

—Fr. Paul Scalia—
Episcopal Vicar for Clergy and Director of the Permanent Diaconate Formation Program, Diocese of Arlington, VA

"*The Last Homily* is a treasure. In one moment you are privy to a fascinating, wide-ranging conversation with a dear friend, and in the next you realize you are sitting at the feet of a spiritual master intent on helping you discover the Father's embrace. Fr. Arne was a gift to those who knew him. I hope many more will come to know him and, through him, to know the Lord."

—Mary Rice Hasson—
Director of the Catholic Women's Forum, Kate O'Beirne Fellow in Catholic Studies, Ethics and Public Policy Center, Washington, DC

"The truest kind of faith is reasonable, coherent, and beautiful. The best witnesses to faith are humble, thoughtful, and real. *The Last Homily* is a kind of holy *apologia*—a witness to true faith in the heart of authentic humanity. Mary Eberstadt has drawn the best from the mind and heart of Fr. Arne Panula, and we are all the better for it."

—J.D. Flynn—
Editor-in-Chief of Catholic News Agency

THE LAST HOMILY

THE LAST HOMILY

Conversations with Fr. Arne Panula

Edited, with an Introduction, by
MARY EBERSTADT

Foreword by GEORGE WEIGEL

Cover art: Portrait of Fr. Arne Panula by
IGOR V. BABAILOV, HON. RAA, KStA

EMMAUS
ROAD
PUBLISHING

Steubenville, Ohio
www.emmausroad.org

Emmaus Road Publishing
1468 Parkview Circle
Steubenville, Ohio 43952

© 2018 Taberg Productions, LLC
All rights reserved. Published 2018
Printed in the United States of America

Library of Congress Cataloging-in-Publication Data

Names: Panula, Arne, interviewee. | Eberstadt, Mary, editor, writer of introduction. | Weigel, George, 1951- writer of foreword.

Title: The last homily : conversations with Fr. Arne Panula / edited and with introduction by Mary Eberstadt ; foreword by George Weigel.

Description: Steubenville, Ohio : Emmaus Road Publishing, 2018.

Identifiers: LCCN 2018033160 (print) | LCCN 2018042803 (ebook) | ISBN 9781949013023 (ebook) | ISBN 9781949013009 | ISBN 9781949013009 (hard cover) | ISBN 9781949013016(paperback)

Subjects: LCSH: Panula, Arne--Interviews. | Priests--United States--Interviews. | Catholic Church--Clergy--Interviews. | LCGFT: Interviews.

Classification: LCC BX4705.P3727 (ebook) | LCC BX4705.P3727 A5 2018 (print) | DDC 282.092 [B] --dc23

LC record available at https://lccn.loc.gov/2018033160

Cover art: *Portrait of Fr. Arne Panula*
by Igor V. Babailov, Hon. RAA, KStA

Cover design and layout by Margaret Ryland

To the converts, reverts, and other stalwart faithful
who are building the Church of tomorrow.

Table of Contents

Fr. Arne Panula and the Easter Effect

Every year, the celebration of Easter reminds us that the Church begins with *witness*: lives changed by an encounter with the Risen Lord; men and women who then transform others by the power of their testimony and the authority of their example.

The Gospels are remarkably candid about the difficulty the first Christian witnesses had in grasping just what they had experienced. In John's gospel, Mary confuses the Risen One with a gardener. In Luke's Resurrection account, two disciples walk a considerable distance on the Emmaus Road without recognizing their risen and glorified companion. In the Johannine epilogue, seven apostles on the Sea of Tiberias take a while to grasp that it's the Risen Lord who's cooking breakfast for them on the seashore.

This candor about incomprehension bears its own witness to the historicity of the Resurrection. For what happened on the first Easter Sunday was so completely unexpected, and yet so completely real, that it exploded the expectations of pious Jews about history, the Messiah, and the fulfillment of God's promises, even as it transformed hitherto timid follow-ers of the Rabbi Jesus of Nazareth into zealous evangelists who set off from the edges of the Roman Empire to convert, over the next two hundred fifty years, perhaps half the Mediterranean world.

The witness of radically converted lives has been the lifeblood of Christianity ever since, for at the bottom of the bottom line of Christian faith is the encounter with a person, the Risen Lord, Jesus Christ. Christianity is also about creed, doctrine, morals, worship, and all the rest. But as Pope Benedict XVI never tired of saying, Christianity is, first and foremost, about friendship with Jesus Christ and the transformation that engenders. And when it ceases to be that, it becomes a lifeless institutional husk (as is sadly the case with much of organized Christianity in Western Europe). Where Christianity lives today, against all cultural odds, it's because of witnesses like those initially confused souls in Judea and Galilee whose conversion began with life-shattering and life-changing encounters with the Risen One.

Which brings me to the man I often called "my favorite Finno-American priest," Father Arne Panula.

A 1967 graduate of Harvard College, young Arne Panula took a doctorate in theology at the University of Navarre in Pamplona, Spain, before ordination as a priest of the Prelature of Opus Dei. After a distinguished career as an elementary school, high school, and college chaplain and service to his religious community, Father Arne Panula was named the Director of the Catholic Information Center [CIC] in Washington, DC, in 2007—an oasis of the spirit located right in the belly of the beast (or, if you prefer, smack-dab in the depths of The Swamp): on K Street between 15th and 16th Streets, surrounded by lobbyists, lawyers, and campaign consultants. And for a decade, from his CIC perch, "Father Arne," as he was known to one and all, became a singularly winsome and effective witness to Christ and an exceptionally dynamic builder of Christian community.

Throughout his ministry in the nation's capital, Father Arne Panula gathered around himself what the Letter to the Hebrews calls a "great cloud of witnesses," whom he then sent out, *urbi et orbi*, to convert the city and the world. His long, heroic, and uncomplaining battle against cancer became his last great teaching moment, a living homily about faith, hope, and priestly charity preached in real time (and often in real pain) by a man who had long ago put himself in the hands of the Risen Lord. And when the time for his Passover came—happily, after he had completed this remarkable series of conversations with Mary Eberstadt—those who loved him and shared his Easter faith knew that it was less a matter of losing a friend than of gaining an intercessor.

There has been a lot of talk by Rod Dreher and others about a "Benedict Option" in recent years, suggesting a certain withdrawal from public life for the sake of forming intentional communities of character. Benedictine monasteries were crucial in preserving the cultural memory of the West during the so-called Dark Ages, and over time became centers of learning and scholarship, prayer and work, that were instrumental in building the civilization of the High Middle Ages. It seems to me that another promising image for what the committed Christian should pursue in the twenty-first century is a "Gregorian Option": building or strengthening intentional communities of character as launchpads for witness, mission, and evangelization. Pope St. Gregory the Great sent the man we now know as St. Augustine of Canterbury to evangelize heathen England—and did so from the Benedictine monastery Gregory had founded in Rome.

For ten years, the Catholic Information Center lived this Gregorian Option under Father Arne Panula, who became the living embodiment in an often smugly secular city of what St. John Paul II called the "New Evangelization." Now, under Father Arne's protection and under the leadership of those he inspired and trained, CIC is living the truth of what Catholicism has been called: "a Church permanently in mission." That happened, and continues to happen, because Father Arne, much like those witnesses the Church reads about in the Gospels and the Acts of the Apostles, had met the Risen Lord. And that, as these conversations make winsomely clear, made all the difference.

George Weigel is Distinguished Senior Fellow of Washington's Ethics and Public Policy Center, where he holds the William E. Simon Chair in Catholic Studies. This foreword was adapted from an article he published in 2017 in National Review. *Used with permission.*

Introduction

The subject of this book is Fr. Arne Panula, a Roman Catholic priest and spiritual mentor who was beloved by a great many people both inside the capital of the United States and out. These pages, which he reviewed and approved, record our conversations between February and June 2017, before his death from cancer on July 19 of that year at age 71.

This "Fr. Arne," as known to all, was a priest in full. His is not—yet—a household name. It would shock no one who knew him if that relative obscurity were someday to change.

Born and raised in Duluth, Minnesota, and educated first at Harvard and later at Spain's University of Navarre, Fr. Arne would go on to spend decades in California, New York, and Washington, DC, working with students and young professionals, financiers, and political leaders, rich and poor, in a variety of settings. By virtue of two appointments, in particular, his spiritual reach would expand across the country and beyond: as Vicar of the Prelature of Opus Dei in the United States between 1998 and 2002; and as Director of the Catholic Information Center in downtown Washington, DC, from 2007–2017.

It was this latter missionary work, in the nation's capital, that brought him to especially wide notice. There, in the business district packed with lawyers and lobbyists, he presided

with infectious *élan* over the blandly named Catholic Information Center—a social, spiritual, and intellectual powerhouse,
set squarely on DC's K Street.

The closest tabernacle to the White House, the CIC
is also a resource like no other: part bookstore, part salon,
part lecture series, and more. Like his predecessors Fr. C. J.
McCloskey and Msgr. William Stetson and his successor
Fr. Charles Trullols, with the aid of a dedicated team led by
COO Mitchell Boersma, Fr. Arne leveraged the CIC's key
location such that pilgrims of every kind ended up migrating
to the place: senators and Supreme Court Justices; tourists
and browsers of books; young professionals; street people;
troubled spirits in search of help; and other wanderers, religious and secular alike. Such is the gravitational pull of the
CIC that many entered, and still do, without an inkling of
what they're seeking. For ten years, Fr. Arne was there to help
them to figure it out.

*   *   *

To grasp the irony that resulted in this book, it helps to
know that Fr. Arne was first and foremost an unapologetic
believer in Providence: the idea that a benevolent God not
only cares about human affairs but also intervenes to shape
them. Beginning with his doctoral dissertation, which cen-
tered on the role of Providence in the theological work of the
great nineteenth-century convert and intellectual Cardinal
John Henry Newman, Fr. Arne saw the hand of God all over.

Well, that Providence he insisted upon has its droll side.
This book wouldn't exist but for an exercise in gallows humor
in 2009. At the time, a eulogy I'd written for an admired

mentor had just been published.[1] Shortly afterwards, I met up with Fr. Arne at one of the CIC's evening book salons. "I like the way you write about your dead friends!" he said by way of greeting. "Will you write about me, too, when I die?" "Only if you promise to write about me, if I go first," I countered. "Deal!" he answered with a great laugh. And so was born our inside joke, which we called the Obituary Pact—an irreverent nod to the tradition of *memento mori*, which remained a source of amusement.

That was before the diagnosis of Stage Four prostate cancer was delivered to Fr. Arne in 2016. Following months during which he nevertheless continued to work full-time on ambitious projects, he was finally dispatched by his doctors to hospice care in winter 2017, right before Lent. Like many other friends, I dropped by during that first week for what we believed could be a final visit—only to have Fr. Arne bring up the Obituary Pact once more. "It's time to take out your notebook and make good on our deal," he said with a grin. Hoping to record a few of his final thoughts for the benefit of those who knew him—and even more for those who hadn't—I started taking notes.

Then Providence threw another curveball. Contrary to forecasts, Fr. Arne ended up living not days or weeks, but several months longer than statistics would have predicted. Throughout, he radiated vigor impossible to square with the knowledge that death cells had taken up residence all over inside. "I'm dying," he reported a few weeks before the end, "And I'm enjoying some of the best hours of my life." This stay of execution, along with his serenity, seemed further confirmation to many onlookers of qualities rarely encountered in life's

---

[1] "My Irving Kristol and Ours," *The Weekly Standard*, October 5, 2009.

ordinary rounds. It also meant more time to try and capture, however necessarily in miniature, the final thoughts of a prodigious leader.

And so, instead of one last conversation that could be mined to make good on our Obituary Pact, I was privileged to enjoy some dozen-plus more with him—enough that there developed sufficient material for this short book. Every few days, amid the steady flow of his other visitors, we'd meet and talk for an hour or more. Each time, I'd transcribe my notes while they were freshly in mind and sketch out other ground to cover next. From Fr. Arne's perspective, only one requirement mattered: "Just don't publish it till after I'm dead," he requested, "so that no one will think I'm self-promoting."

*   *   *

It's the premise of this project that even those with no religious conviction will find in the dying thoughts of this priest a great deal upon which to reflect. Here is a man of many talents, captivating social presence, and formidable intellect. He could have become a scientist, a businessman, a professor, a university president, a politician. Instead, Arne Panula threw his life at God.

Throughout, Providence proved an ironist. A math and science *wunderkind*, the future priest nevertheless graduated from Harvard University an English major, with a lifelong devotion to Shakespeare and Keats; the resulting sharp feel for language would later prove to be one of the surgical tools in his religious conversion kit. Educated in elite secular venues, and surrounded by worldly friends, he nonetheless went all-in for the Church, being ordained in 1973. Handsome, and bearing an uncanny resemblance to the young Karol

Wojtyla, he would go on to witness to many people—especially young people—that their souls depended on what was beautiful inside, not outside.

How could a product of elite, secular education retain such faith in a secular time? What kind of advice about life and work, love and marriage, sanctity and sin, did he deliver to the many people who sought him out during decades as a spiritual director? How can modern men and women find holiness in an unholy world?

These are just some of the questions upon which the late Fr. Arne meditates in the pages ahead, as death loitered somewhere around the corner. Cicero, followed by Montaigne, held that to philosophize is to learn how to die. Sitting with Fr. Arne during those hospice weeks and months meant learning something else: to die well is to teach others how to live.

It was our joint hope that these last teachings will live on not only to comfort his friends and followers, who will find here a microcosm of what made them cherish him; but also that this book would reach other people, including and especially the secular-minded, who will find in these pages a portrait of a religious mind thoroughly out of step with secularist caricature, including though not only for its intellectual sophistication. By way of example, notes from one of our last conversations alone include his references to works by Henri du Lubac, René Girard, Hans Urs von Balthasar, Cardinal Francis George, Archbishop Charles J. Chaput, and Cardinal Robert Sarah—and that was in an hour before lunch. Readers will also find nods to Shakespeare and Keats, Dickens and Eliot, music and art, and other grace notes of a cultivated mind. One of the CIC's offerings is a lifetime reading list. To sit with Fr. Arne toward the end was to fast-forward through lots of it.

He was also an athlete and devoted gardener—a Renaissance man who, amusingly enough, found many of the most famous paintings from that era over-the-top and ostentatious. Stopping by for one of our last conversations, I found him poring through a box of small papers with pictures on them. "I hope you don't think I'm being macabre," he said, "but I'm picking out the illustration for my funeral cards, and it's frustrating. All of the paintings are masterpieces from the Renaissance! I can't find anything simple enough."

Fr. Arne no more flaunted his learning than he did his spiritual workings among powerful men and women in Washington and elsewhere. But for idea-dropping, he couldn't be beat—which is why readers with no interest in the "Catholic thing" can nonetheless find plenty else on which to ruminate here.

*　　*　　*

On a technical note: the conversations in these pages were *actual* conversations, with the ebbs and flows that spontaneous exchange implies. That is to say, they are not pre-recorded interviews, nor questions and answers passed back and forth via email, but real live discussions, transcribed from handwritten notes, aided in some cases by smartphone recording, and edited only minimally. The quotations from books and articles were also part of our conversations, called up on our phones as we were talking. Footnotes were added later, for readers who may be interested in learning more.

These talks transpired either in the drawing room at Fr. Arne's residence in downtown Washington, or, weather permitting, in the garden outside. Typically, I'd enter having only scribbled down a few themes to cover that day—*books, music, architecture; rules to live by, love and marriage; secularization, theodicy*—minimal prompts that were all he needed to get started. From there, improvisation ruled. And necessarily so, since we never knew from one conversation to the next which would be the last.

In addition to the Foreword by George Weigel, this book includes as an Appendix a compilation of recollections and anecdotes by other friends, desiring to capture thoughts of their own for the record.

* * *

A few months before he entered hospice care, some friends commissioned a portrait of Fr. Arne from renowned artist Igor Babailov. It was characteristic that the subject would assent to a charcoal portrait only; any rendering in color, he feared, would have seemed immodest.

While the artist was working on this piece, one of many in his studio in Tennessee, his wife Mary told friends a story that soon made the rounds of Washington. "I always go to the studio, to look at what Igor's up to," she reported. "There's one portrait he's doing now that I can't stop staring at. I've never known that DC priest he's drawing. But I cannot shake the feeling I have every time I'm drawn to it: This must be a truly holy man."[2]

Many who knew Fr. Arne will be nodding, upon reading those words. Within these final conversations, one of the most piercing moments for me occurred when he was talking one

---

[2] This story was relayed by Mary Babailov on February 25, 2017, at a reception following the funeral of theologian Michael Novak. Igor Babailov himself, who did not know Fr. Arne until this commission, further reports that the priest's portrait sitting was one of the two most emotional experiences he had ever had of a subject. The other was his experience of painting John Paul II, as pope.

morning about St. Josemaría Escrivá, founder of Opus Dei, whom he'd known before becoming a priest. "Everyone wanted to know the same thing when he was canonized," Fr. Arne said casually. "Everyone asked the same question of me: Did you ever think you'd known a saint?"

May the pages ahead give readers a sense of Fr. Arne's extraordinary personality, his unmistakable joy all the way to the finish line, and his boundless faith in a God who provides for his unknowing children—even in the improbable form of an Obituary Pact, about which he continued to joke mischievously during hours that number among the most incandescent of this unexpected interlocutor's life.

—*Mary Eberstadt*
Washington, DC
May 2018

1

Let's Begin at the Beginning . . .

FEBRUARY 2017

Fr. Arne, we've spoken of the hope that these last reflections of yours will reach secular as well as religious readers. So let's start with a couple of questions that are bound to be on the minds of people outside church circles. Why do you believe in God?

Fr. Arne: Often people say, you only believe all that because you're Catholic. My response is, no, I'm Catholic because I believe all that.

Begin with the human hunger to drill into reality. It's a constant of our lives. As you dig, you uncover different paradigms. Which fits best with all that you know about the world, about people, about life itself?

Or to switch metaphors: coming to belief is like going to an ophthalmologist and trying different lenses on your eyes. You know that feeling of *bingo!* when the right one fits. When you couple the experience of life with the right rendering, you find what fits. This is one reason why I read the New Testament a little, every day, and have been for fifty years. Every day, I find new things in the faith. Every day, the picture gets sharper. Now obviously, there's a "gifted-ness" to all these experiences. It's not as if I've done this all by myself—or even could. The grace needed to stick with the project is also God-given. Believing in God is a collaboration. God doesn't force us to do it. But that's what makes faith an adventure. Emeritus Pope Benedict has said: we believe in someone, not something.[1] Thomas Aquinas says similarly in the *Summa theologica* that the object of our belief is not a dogma, but a person. That's what makes faith fascinating. All the adventure, all the mystery of any and every interpersonal encounter is there.

Are you always equally aware of the other person?

Fr. Arne: Definitely not. The awareness comes and goes. That's why doctrine is so important. It gives you something to hold onto when the sense of the interpersonal isn't as present.

By nature we are solipsistic. It's easy to get sucked into avoiding God. This is as true for priests as for everyone else. St. Josemaría Escrivá tells a story about sitting in the confessional during the mornings. Every day, he'd hear the church door bang open, then the clanging of cans, then another slamming shut of the doors. Curious, he stationed himself one morning on the church steps and came face-to-face at the appointed hour with a milkman, carrying his cans into the church. He asked the man what he was doing, and the milkman answered: "Father, every day I come here, open the door, and say 'Hello, Jesus! Here's John the milkman.'"

---

[1] Benedict XVI, *Deus Caritas Est*, December 25, 2005, available from http://w2.vatican.va/content/benedict-xvi/en/encyclicals/documents/hf_ben-xvi_enc_20051225_deus-caritas-est.html.

The priest was speechless. He spent the rest of the day asking in prayer for the faith of John the milkman.[2]

There's a story in similar spirit that a friend relayed a few years ago. A priest in Ohio walked into his church and saw a lone man on his knees in the pews. The priest recognized him as a famous football player—one of the best-known in the NFL, in town for a game that day. Unable to resist, the priest approached and said, "Aren't you so-and-so?" To which the athlete looked up and corrected him with, "Father, I'm praying."

Fr. Arne: Yes, the point of both stories is the tangible faith in the presence of God, and how easy it is to get distracted from that.

Even so, and even when the interpersonal nature of faith ebbs and flows, grace abounds, and its presence has an effect on faith all its own. To see grace at work, as I have for forty-four years of priestly spiritual direction, is remarkable. My faith is affirmed constantly by those observations alone.

Especially for nonreligious readers: what's meant by grace, and where does it show itself?

Fr. Arne: Grace is visible, first, in the transformation that takes place over time in an individual first coming to belief. As people begin to practice the faith, to pray, to meditate on its truths, they change visibly.

I've seen it constantly. People actually practicing the faith find themselves growing in patience and in wonder. Another singular fact one notices is the expansion of their capacity for

---

[2] Vázquez de Prada, *The Founder of Opus Dei: The Life of Josemaría Escrivá*, vol. 1 (Dublin: Four Courts, 2001), 387.

joy. It's not that they become mystical, or otherwise vanish into the religious ether. It's quite the opposite: their energy becomes much more focused.

Another manifestation of grace is that people on the religious road also grow in interest and concern for others. Their selflessness increases. I see this, too, all the time. It's more evidence of the transformative power of grace.

Here's another question asked often by people who aren't yet on that road. What's the importance of going to church, as opposed to "just being spiritual"?

Fr. Arne: When people talk about being "spiritual" as opposed to religious, they're talking about their personal experience of God—period.

But God created us as social animals. We need to be connected to one another.

The early Christian community, on being told to celebrate the Eucharist in memory of Jesus, developed rituals. These were practiced in community. There's a great book by Brant Pitre called *Jesus and the Jewish Roots of the Eucharist,* showing how Mass developed out of the Sabbath.[3] And there is also St. John Paul II's wonderful 1998 Apostolic Letter—*Dies Domini* (*The Day of the Lord*): *On Keeping the Lord's Day Holy,* which draws a thread through the Day of Creation, to the Day of Redemption in Christ, to the Day of the Church, to the Day of Eternity.[4]

---

[3] Brant Pitre, *Jesus and the Jewish Roots of the Eucharist: Unlocking the Secrets of the Last Supper* (New York: Image, 2011).

[4] *Dies Domini,* July 30, 1998, available from https://w2.vatican.va/content/ john-paul-ii/en/apost_letters/1998/documents/hf_jp-ii_apl_05071998_ dies-domini.htmlhttps://w2.vatican.va/content/john-paul-ii/en/ apost_letters/1998/documents/hf_jp-ii_apl_05071998_dies-domini.html.

The idea that there's a special day to rest, worship, be with family and in community, isn't just some arbitrary quirk; it conforms to human nature—it's something that human beings repeatedly reveal themselves to want. Similarly, the whole idea of the Liturgy of the Word is drawn from Jewish tradition. We don't exist as social isolates, but as beings who live in community and who practice things that only make sense in community. Worship is one of them.

In his History of Christianity, *twentieth-century Yale historian Kenneth Scott Latourette makes a similar point about community.[5] He asks how the faith could possibly have spread in just a few hundred years from a handful of bedraggled followers into a religion that would spread as far as Central Asia, India and Ceylon, north to Ireland, and the rest of the map of its flourishing.*

Some assume the answer is that Emperor Constantine adopted the faith, and everyone else fell into line. But as Latourette points out, that can't be so; Christianity had already spread across the Roman Empire without political help, indeed, despite centuries of persecution by the state itself.

Latourette argues instead that Christianity delivered what people were looking for better than its rivals did. In particular, its strict moral code set the religion apart, and gave people a stringent standard to which to aspire; and its extraordinary degree of fellowship made it stand out. This was manifest not only in the martyrs who went peacefully to their deaths, certain of their places in the Christian community; but also of the traditions established early on for taking care of the sick, the weak, the aged, the helpless.

---

5   Kenneth Scott Latourette, *A History of Christianity, Volume I: Beginnings to 1500,* rev. ed. (New York: Harper and Row, 1953; repr. 1975).

The bottom line would appear to be: no community, no Christianity.[6]

Fr. Arne: We aren't meant to be atomized creatures. We want to share our beliefs, our feelings, our thoughts, our hopes. This is especially true of our deepest, most cherished convictions— our beliefs about what's most important.

Being in St. Peter's Square, whether for Mass or anything else, is so very different from hearing the Beatles in Central Park. Both are obviously venues for large numbers of people, united by something. But in St. Peter's Square, what's uniting people is a hub; and not just any hub, but one that transcends the merely human. When people feel transcendence, they want to share it with others; they want to *be* with others.

I like to compare the faith to a game of galactic tag. Someone who's "it" touches another, and then the other has "it" too, and goes on to touch others. You can't play tag alone.

---

[6] Latourette summarizes:

"Better than its rivals, Christianity gave to the Graeco-Roman world what so many were craving from a religion. To those wishing immortality it pointed to the historic Jesus, risen from the dead, and to the promise that those who believed in him would share in glorified, eternal life. To those demanding high morality it offered standards beyond the full attainment of men and the power to grow towards them. To those craving fellowship it presented a community of worship and of mutual aid, with care for the poor, the infirm, and the aged. To those who, distrustful of reason, longed for a faith sanctioned by immemorial antiquity, it pointed to the long record preserved in what it termed the Old Testament, going back to Moses and beyond him and pointing forward to Christ. To those demanding intellectual satisfaction it could present literature prepared by some of the ablest minds of the day" (*History of Christianity, vol. 1*, 107).

Ludwig Wittgenstein observed that there can be no such thing as a private language, because language requires community—even presupposes it. The very idea of "private" religion seems logically impossible as well.

Fr. Arne: This is why the popular notion of being "just spiritual" is ultimately unsustainable. Yet still, Millennials especially are drawn to it—in part because atomization is so characteristic of their age.

I was just reading a reflection by Peter Lawler in *Public Discourse*, meditating thirty years later on Allan Bloom's thesis in *Closing of the American Mind*.[7] He's illuminating on exactly this point about the atomization of today's world, especially among the young, and how unnatural it is.

Lawler uses the phrase "social solitaries" to describe the children of today's secularized elite—the next generation from the one described by Bloom. He writes: "They think of themselves as self-sufficient wholes. How can an individual be a whole? Only by being without the longing for relational love and by being unmoved by the invincible fact of personal extinction."

That nails it, I think.

Science has documented so much lately about the inner workings of animals, who are social creatures, too. It's ironic that we do understand the social nature of mammals . . . all other mammals, that is. You can't buy a single female gerbil from a pet store, for instance; it will die in isolation from others. One reason why circuses are shutting down is that evidence shows how dependent elephants are

---

7   Peter Augustine Lawler, "Allan Bloom's Souls without Longing, All Grown Up," *Public Discourse*, May 23, 2017.

on thriving in the company of other elephants—in elephant community, as it were.

These scientific findings may seem obvious by now. But when it comes to human beings, somehow we think that isolation is going to work out for us—even as atomization remains something we wouldn't wish on other animals, because we understand it would amount to cruelty.

Fr. Arne: If we were to try to tweak the natural physical world the way we now try to tweak human nature, we'd not only destroy the world in a week, but the universe. There's extraordinary order throughout the physical world, as scientists know. Yet somehow we human beings think we're different, exceptional, immune to the rules about what we are.

It's so ironic, in a profound way, when people say that the Church just wants to restrict human freedom. The truth is that God has created us free—so free that we can even endanger ourselves—and if we violate the boundaries, pretend that our nature is something other than it is, we can hurt ourselves and others.

And we have plenty of leeway to do it. Anyone who doubts that human freedom extends to destroying ourselves might keep in mind the Darwin Awards.[8]

---

[8] As Wikipedia reports, the Darwin Awards "recognize individuals who have supposedly contributed to human evolution by selecting themselves out of the gene pool via death or sterilization by their own actions. The project became more formalized with the creation of a website in 1993, and followed up by a series of books starting in 2000, authored by Wendy Northcutt."

2

Why the Priesthood?

Here's another question of likely interest to secular and religious readers alike. How and why did you end up becoming a priest?

Fr. Arne: I don't have a spiel. My father was not Catholic. He wasn't anything—Lutheran Finnish. He converted when I was in Rome. My mother's maiden name was Bellinger— Welsh-Scottish. Ours wasn't particularly a pious home. We said grace, prayed the Rosary for a year or two, went to Mass. My father would drive us, because mother didn't drive. I have three sisters—an older, a twin, and a younger; and a brother who died in childbirth.

I started serving Mass in middle school. The pastor offered to send me to St. Thomas Seminary in Minnesota. My academic strengths were in math and science; a good friend of my father had gone to MIT, and that became my aspiration. Politics never interested me. My parents were both Democrats; I always disdained politics. Between my junior and senior year of high school I went to Corvalis, Oregon, for a six-week program, National Science Foundation; and the following summer, to a similar program at University of Minnesota.

That was an intellectual awakening, and not because of the science. We'd stay up till 2:00 in the morning, talking about life, etc. I made a number of good friendships. In the fall I applied to MIT, University of Chicago, and Harvard. The Harvard catalog was of interest for offering the greatest breadth [beyond the sciences], so I accepted and started in the fall of 1963. Two friends of mine also went to Harvard.

My undergraduate career was mixed. I did quite well my freshman year and received honors. Harvard was another great awakening, a whole world I was little familiar with.

What set did you run with?

Fr. Arne: [laughs] I dressed like the preppie crowd. Other students wondered if I'd gone to Groton. I was bedazzled with Harvard's old world.

Where does Opus Dei enter the story?

Fr. Arne: My older sister went to study at Michigan Tech, and when I visited her during her first year there she showed me the Catholic student center—chapel, library, resident chaplain. She and I were intellectually the closest of the siblings, and I knew right away that I wanted something similar wherever I might go to study. Later at Harvard, after Sunday Mass, the school cafeteria was closed; so I'd end up in the Catholic coffee place. I met a Filipino grad student who told me of a place with a chapel and fellowship with others. He was also talking with a number of others from South America, and at first I thought this was too international a crowd for me. But as I was leaving, he stopped me, and eventually we walked over to Elmbrook Residence at the opposite side of campus. It seemed like a good place to study, so I started hanging around. I had no plan of becoming a priest, not then. But the idea of sanctity in the everyday things of the world—a pillar of St. Josemaría's spiritual thought—was one I found deeply attractive. The day after Kennedy was assassinated, my Filipino friend suggested that I join Opus Dei.

As of my sophomore year, I had a profound sense that something was wrong. It seemed to me that Harvard was full of intellectual glibness. At the time, I was reading in the philosophy of history, which moved me to study more in the fields of history and English; and English literature became my major, despite my longer-standing foundations in math and science.

In retrospect, something else telling happened that year. I was assistant manager of the Harvard crew team, and there was a young fellow on it with whom I'd talk about English lit. He ended up dropping out, and the next year I saw him in uniform. He was killed in Vietnam.

It bothered me that I hadn't talked to him more deeply about faith. I wondered whether that might have made a difference to where he ended up after death. That was my first conscious thought of spiritual fatherhood.

I was living in Eliot House and having conversations, and sometimes arguments, with a wonderful rotating set of characters. Still, my studies had ceased commanding my full attention; the feeling that something was wrong at Harvard, and elsewhere in the sophisticated world, preoccupied me. By senior year, I had developed the game plan of going to Harvard Business School. I thought I'd become an investment banker, a pinstripes guy.

But then one of the regional directors of Opus Dei suggested that I go to Rome on a fellowship. I liked the idea. I got into business school as planned, but deferred.

It was 1967—the so-called "summer of love." I ended up staying in Europe for two years studying philosophy and theology, mostly in Paris, Rome, and in a little town in the Apennines. Ultimately, I ended up staying in Europe for six and a half years—passing through Paris, living in Rome for two years to study philosophy and theology, and then studying in Pamplona, Spain, where I finished my doctoral dissertation. This inoculated me for good against the druggie-hippie culture of those years, but I still wasn't drawn to the priesthood. Then I met St. Josemaría shortly after arriving in Rome.

What were your first impressions of him?

Fr. Arne: He had a great sense of love of God; a great sense of humor; he was very strong, despite the pain that he suffered because of the way the Church was being torn apart from within following the Second Vatican Council.

I asked him once: "Father, what do you think of the new liturgy?" There was a pregnant pause, and he replied, "I will obey."

That was a significant moment for me. I was impressed by his strength of character and his obedience at the same time. He had great intelligence, great wit, and great affection for us. He could move from the sublime to the ridiculous quickly. I felt a deepening appreciation of the title by which we called him: "Father."

Then I went to Spain, University of Navarre in Pamplona, to finish classes and undertake a doctorate. I still thought I would return to the States as a layman. I attended a forty-day, intense Opus Dei program in the south of Spain. It's a long seminar, like Tertio Millennio in Krakow.[1] At the end, the director asked if I'd head a men's residence at the University of Navarre, and I said, sure.

Dealing with the headaches and heartaches of all those guys touched a deep pastoral nerve, and moved me to think of becoming a priest. I consulted with St. Josemaría. He told me to pray about it and six months later, I told him I'd made the decision. I was ordained at the Basilica of St. Michael in Madrid in August 1973.

What was your dissertation about?

Fr. Arne: It concerned the works of Cardinal John Henry Newman—about how Providence turns the heart and head at least as much as ideas do. It's about how Providence sometimes pushes us along and becomes a force in itself.[2]

Besides becoming a priest, what else did you learn from those years in Europe?

Fr. Arne: They taught me that what was missing from modern life is a whole metaphysical understanding of objective reality.

Back in Cambridge, MA, one day, I came across a leaded window with the Harvard seal on it: *Veritas Christo et Ecclesiae*

---

[1] The Tertio Millennio Seminar on the Free Society is a three-week program of study that takes place annually in Krakow, Poland. It was founded in 1992 by Michael Novak, Rocco Buttiglione, Fr. Richard John Neuhaus, Fr. Maciej Zieba, OP, and George Weigel for the purpose of deepening the dialogue on Catholic social doctrine between North American students and others from the democracies of central and eastern Europe.

[2] Editor's note: an expanded discussion of the dissertation follows later, in Conversation 14.

(Truth for Christ and the Church). I thought, if the seal has already lost *Christo* and *Ecclesiae*, can *Veritas* be far behind?[3]

---

[3] Editor's note: for background on the Harvard seal and the diminishing of public Christianity on campus, see Anna K. Kendrick, "Harvard's Secularization," The Crimson, March 8, 2006.

3

Reading Books and Reading People

Editor's note: The following conversation took place in the drawing room on Ash Wednesday, March 1, 2017 on a humid, gray day in Washington, DC.

Fr. Arne, as someone who's surrounded by authors and their works, what books have you found essential?

Fr. Arne: You know, it's funny. I live in a bookstore and look out on these books longingly. But I really read people.

In the matter of reading books instead . . . David Perkins, the darling of the Harvard English department, gave a course on Shakespeare, Keats, and Eliot. Those are three authors I read and re-read ever since. I was taken by the Romantics. I could read Keats forever. And Shakespeare.

Perkins's point was that these authors were rooted in reality. In retrospect, you could see the metaphysical bug gnawing at me, by the early attraction to these authors.

What are some of your favorite works?

Fr. Arne: In Shakespeare, *King Lear, Henry IV*, the sonnets, *Hamlet.*

I learned Latin in order to read Aquinas in the original. The standard translation has the inconvenience that relative pronouns can lead you all over the place. I took classes in Latin for that reason, before becoming a priest.

What about other languages?

Fr. Arne: I used to be quite fluent in Spanish. I can read French and Italian. Unfortunately I never got into Finnish, which is related to Basque. My father could speak Finnish, but didn't pass that down.

What about contemporary writers?

Fr. Arne: For philosophy and theology, Josef Pieper and Joseph Ratzinger. Another area I've been intensely interested in is Christology, the branch of theology concerning the nature and person of Christ.

Bob [Fr. Robert] Barron's book *The Priority of Christ* is very good, very scriptural.[1] Gil Bailie's *Violence Unveiled*, about René Girard's thought, is another excellent example.[2] Girard himself thought this the best *precis* of his work. Gil was doing a road series, giving brilliant lectures around the country about other influential figures, like Henri de Lubac

---

[1] Fr. Robert Barron, *The Priority of Christ: Toward a Postliberal Catholicism* (Grand Rapids, MI: Baker Academic, 2016).

[2] Gil Bailie, *Violence Unveiled: Humanity at the Crossroads* (New York: Crossroad, 1996).

and Hans Urs von Balthasar. I encouraged him to write a book that came out last fall entitled *God's Gamble: The Gravitational Pull of Crucified Love*.[3]

And of course you and I and many more readers are great fans of Archbishop [Charles J.] Chaput and the late Cardinal Francis George, two of the best churchmen writing in our time. Other intellectual leaders among our friends include George Weigel and Michael Novak. Recently I've been reading and admiring Cardinal [Robert] Sarah's *God or Nothing*.[4] He's a wonderful man—humble, holy, bright. Brad Gregory's *The Unintended Reformation* traces the roots of modernity back to the fourteenth century, and shows the unraveling of metaphysical thought that so deeply impacts modernity.[5]

What about contemporary secular thinkers—any favorites there?

Fr. Arne: None has made a deep and lasting impression.

During my California years, I was mostly living outdoors and shepherding high school students—not really conducive to deep thinking. I always found myself in long conversations with Peter Thiel, who founded the contrarian *Stanford Review* during the era when students chanted "Hey, hey, ho ho—Western civ has got to go!" We don't see eye to eye on everything, but we've been serious intellectual friends for almost thirty years now, and I always benefit from talking to Peter—it's like sharpening steel on steel. But there weren't many others of that caliber who had the necessary energy or

[3] Gil Bailie, *God's Gamble: The Gravitational Pull of Crucified Love* (Brooklyn, NY: Angelico Press, 2016).

[4] Cardinal Robert Sarah, *God or Nothing: A Conversation on Faith* (San Francisco: Ignatius, 2015).

[5] Brad S. Gregory, *The Unintended Reformation: How a Religious Revolution Secularized Society*, 1st ed. (Cambridge, MA: Belknap, 2010).

the intellectual sophistication to engage matters outside their immediate orbit.

In the realm of the written word, I have always found primary sources more engaging and more important. These have been more influential on me than any commentaries.

It's remarkable how many serious and important books have appeared during the last decade alone, assessing the West's spiritual condition and its origins. In addition to those we've already talked about, there's also Robert Royal's A Deeper Vision, *about the Catholic intellectual tradition in the twentieth century; Pierre Manet's* Beyond Radical Secularism; *George Weigel's* The Cube and the Cathedral, *about the civilizational crisis in Europe; wide-ranging diagnoses of the American condition, like Rod Dreher's* The Benedict Option, *Anthony Esolen's* Up from the Ashes, *and Archbishop Chaput's* Strangers in a Strange Land; *books by outstanding priest scholars, like Fr. Paul Scalia's* That Nothing May Be Lost, *and two guides to the faith by Fr. Roger Landry and Fr. Thomas Joseph White, OP, respectively—this list could go on and on.*[6]

---

[6] Robert Royal, *A Deeper Vision: The Catholic Intellectual Tradition in the Twentieth Century* (San Francisco: Ignatius, 2015); Pierre Manet, *Beyond Radical Secularism: How France and the United States Should Respond to the Islamic Challenge*, trans. Ralph C. Hancock (South Bend, IN: St. Augustine's Press, 2015); George Weigel, *The Cube and the Cathedral: Europe, America, and Politics without God* (New York: Basic Books, 2005); Rod Dreher, *The Benedict Option: A Strategy for Christians in a Post-Christian Nation* (New York: Sentinel, 2017); Anthony Esolen, *Out of the Ashes: Rebuilding American Culture* (Washington, DC: Regnery, 2017); Charles J. Chaput, *Strangers in a Strange Land: Living the Catholic Faith in a Post-Christian World* (New York: Henry Holt and Company, 2017); Paul Scalia, *That Nothing May Be Lost: Reflections on Catholic Doctrine and Devotion* (San Francisco: Ignatius, 2017); Roger J. Landry, *Plan of Life: Habits to Help You Grow Closer to God* (Alexandria, VA: Pauline Books & Media, 2018); Thomas Joseph White, OP, *The Light of Christ: An Introduction to Catholicism* (Washington, DC: Catholic University of America Press, 2017).

Also remarkable, this intellectual outpouring appears practically unknown outside religious circles; secular tastemakers seem not to have noticed. Yet it's hard to believe that this flourishing of the Christian mind will continue in isolation—that intellectual renewal won't give rise to wider renewal.

Are seeds of revival being sown, even amid what seems to be growing hostility toward Christianity itself?

Fr. Arne: The whole idea of George Weigel's "Great Awakening," floated in his 2017 Simon Lecture, is one I've thought of for a long time.[7]

And when it transpires, that, too, will be an example of change being effected by a reckoning with reality. Think of the example of the Leonine Forum.[8] When these twenty-something students, products of what are supposed to be our finest universities, finally get to plumb the reality of two thousand years of the highest intellectual and artistic achievements of humanity, their reaction is twofold: one, an instinctive *wow!* Their next thought is to wonder why these treasures have been deliberately kept from them by the secularist establishment.

---

[7]   The William E. Simon Lecture is delivered annually in Washington, DC, by the Ethics and Public Policy Center's Distinguished Senior Fellow George Weigel. An adapted version of the 2017 Lecture mentioned in the text appears in print as "A New Awakening," *National Affairs* No. 35, Spring 2018, available from https://nationalaffairs.com/publications/detail/a-new-awakening.

[8]   The Leonine Forum, a course of study which brings together young professionals on a monthly basis for intellectual and spiritual exchange, was founded by Fr. Arne and Mitchell Boersma in 2013. Its mission is "to cultivate an emerging generation of virtuous leaders and empower them to form fully integrated lives of faith in order to apply the Social Teachings of the Church within their professional and civic lives." Following the success of the first Forum in Washington, DC, another was founded in New York after Fr. Arne's death; and plans are also underway for a Forum in Los Angeles, as he mentions in the text.

Their example is instructive, again for what it reveals about reality. Once you're bitten by reality, it's like being bitten by intellectual malaria. Eventually it gets to you. It brings out a breakthrough: "eureka!"

Are there any other contemporary texts you recommend to young people who are products of this secular world, which might be conducive to the sort of epiphany you're describing?

Fr. Arne: Cardinal Ratzinger's *Introduction to Christianity* is one I often recommend.[9] It's a heartening, positive vision of the faith that young people find surprising. My image of Ratzinger is a Bavarian tour guide, leading visitors through a castle. You can piece together what he tells you about the extraordinary building you're going through.

He is, to my mind, the consummate pedagogue, never pedantic. He draws you in modestly, gives you a sense of the shared adventure of discovering the Church.

---

[9] Cardinal Joseph Ratzinger, *Introduction to Christianity* (San Francisco: Ignatius, 2004).

4

Some Questions about Opus Dei

Fr. Arne, as you know, I'm not a member of Opus Dei, and for that matter, neither are most of the rest of the people who hang around the CIC—including Mitchell Boersma, who's been your right-hand man for years. Non-Opus Catholics and readers generally will be curious about that part of your story.

For starters, you're a priest of Opus Dei, which is an unusual choice. Most priests are either diocesan or in religious orders. So why Opus Dei?

Fr. Arne: The idea of everyday sanctity, how holiness is possible even in the smallest of things, was a powerful one for me. One thing I always appreciated about Opus Dei was the notion that God resides in the smallest of realities. He doesn't always roar. Sometimes he whispers.

That recalls the passage in Kings, about God coming to Elijah as a light breath.[1] Here's another question that readers might be

---

[1] 1 Kings 19: 11–13: "Then the LORD said: Go out and stand on the mountain before the LORD; the LORD will pass by. There was a strong

wondering. Everyone knows that Opus Dei has become the object of controversy—to say nothing of the ferocious, commercially sensational treatment afforded by Dan Brown and company. Why is Opus Dei such a lightning rod?

Fr. Arne: For one thing, precisely because it seeks realism, not artifice.

Here's a story from my Stanford days. There was a Jesuit on campus, Fr. Russ, who once complained that there were Opus Dei students who didn't identify themselves as such. They dressed like everyone else; studied and otherwise moved around other people in ordinary ways; and yet they remained members of Opus Dei. He seemed to think this amounted to subterfuge.

So we had a meeting to discuss the matter. Fr. Russ was wearing wide-wale corduroy pants and other civilian garb. I was in clerics. I said, "Russ, you're a professed religious, and you go around in mufti; and yet you complain that these lay people are hiding something important. Don't you think that's incongruous?" [laughs]

What about Opus Dei and its perception within the Church itself—any thoughts on that?

Fr. Arne: Many.

The first three centuries of Christianity were chaotic, disorganized, and persecutorial. Then almost overnight, as of the

---

and violent wind rending the mountains and crushing rocks before the LORD—but the LORD was not in the wind; after the wind, an earthquake—but the LORD was not in the earthquake; after the earthquake, fire—but the LORD was not in the fire; after the fire, a light silent sound. When he heard this, Elijah hid his face in his cloak and went out and stood at the entrance of the cave."

Peace of Constantine, the Church went from being persecuted to privileged. This gave rise to a feeling among reformers and would-be reformers that Christianity had gotten too soft, with the result that different solutions were tried over the coming centuries. Cassiodorus and Boethius tried to bring the faith to bear on government, for example. Boethius was sent to prison where he wrote *The Consolation of Philosophy*, and was then beheaded.[2] Meanwhile, Cassiodorus went off to live the Benedict Rule.

For centuries after that, Benedictines and Cistercians kept order, and closed themselves off from the world. Later, into the Middle Ages, come the Franciscans and the Dominicans. All these religious orders were doing critical, vital work. They were also part of what created the sense that holiness was to be found in religious life, cordoned off partly or completely from the rest of the world.

In a very different way, the Jesuits next fed the same narrative via their missionary work. There was the daring evangelization of the New World, most obviously. The Jesuits became the superheroes of evangelization, the new holy religious darlings.

This pattern, in which men of the cloth spearheaded religious outreach, continues for centuries—until 1928, to be exact, when St. Josemaría was struck with a new vision. Until then, the idea prevailed that one could only get on a fast track to heaven by joining a religious order. But the vision he had on October 2, 1928, bore a different message: *everyone* is called to holiness.

---

[2] Boethius, *The Consolation of Philosophy*, trans. Victor Watts, rev. ed. (London: Penguin Classics, 1999).

This was, and is, a controversial idea in some places. St. Josemaría himself was accused of heresy for it. There were organized campaigns against him. St. Josemaría's response was: "Keep quiet, pray, smile, keep on working." He told people not to say a word against anyone.

When God wants to perform a delicate operation, he chooses a platinum scalpel, and St. Josemaría considered those stirring up the opposition to be just that.

What about the secular world? Why does it find Opus Dei so transgressive—so "scary"?

Fr. Arne: It's precisely the witness of all those people next door that makes secular men and women uncomfortable. It's easy for non-religious people to dismiss those in religious orders and monasteries. They're foreign territory, and mostly out of sight. But this Opus Dei spirituality is much closer and more threatening.

And there's something else that's terribly important and sensitive during our broken age. At the heart of Opus Dei is the idea of divine filiation, the notion that God loves each of us as a father loves children.

5

Yearning for the Filial in a Fatherless World

Is that why Opus Dei is a lightning rod? Because it's grounded right in the middle of the world after the sexual revolution—a world in which so many don't know fathers or fatherhood?

Fr. Arne: That's what I think.

A lot of young people ask, what's my vocation? What am I supposed to do?

It would be much easier and simpler if there were some blueprint. But what matters most is to realize that God is a loving father who dotes on seeing how his children will use what he gave them. Of course there are choices that will disappoint him, even as others delight. This whole business of vocation develops as it goes.

Adversity can be a gift in itself, if one looks at it as a tool to be used. Cancer, for example, has become part of my toolkit. The adventure of discovery is daily. I have an amazing sense every day of God being there, but without being obtrusive or oppressive.

The greatest problem I find in young adults today is the fear of being revealed as a fraud. This is part of the lack of filiation, lack of trust.

That same lack of filiation can also be presumed to have some connection to another telling sign of the age, i.e., our angry identity politics. Everyone's obsessed with identity, because the most obvious identity imprints of humanity—our familial markers—are less visible than ever before.

Fr. Arne: Of course. So many people don't even understand what identity is, because they don't understand themselves as children of a family.

Some years back, I was in Fiesole, and I met a young man for coffee who was a friend of a friend. And this young man felt compelled to tell me, "Father, I'm gay." To which I replied: "No, you're not. What you really are is a beloved son of God." I was making the point that *this* was his identity, the most fundamental fact about him—not the fact of his sexual attractions.

Without the filial, both trust and identity become problematic: is that the idea?

Fr. Arne: Yes, it's the ability to trust in a father—or the Father—that reduces anxiety about the future, about work, about vocation. Without that trust, all is fraught.

But with it, the path is such an adventure. In my own life, I've never had a five-year plan or superscript. It's always been going along, with prayer, led by insight in quiet ways. I've always found these more fruitful than being a master of the universe, even for a good cause.

Some would date the rupture of the filial to the invention and dissemination of the birth control pill, leading to unprecedented rates of divorce, abortion, and fatherless homes. Perfectly secular researchers have documented that causal connection. Do you have a different mile marker in mind—or do you think the Pill is it?

Fr. Arne: I agree that the sexual revolution is fundamental here, but also sense that the origins of the filial rupture go further back.

Here's my critique of Tom Brokaw's *The Greatest Generation*, the book and argument according to which the men who were soldiers in World War II went on to become singularly model American citizens.[1] I disagree with that thesis.

All those millions of soldiers came home as ruptured sons. They came back from the war after enduring what they did, and they didn't know how to be fathers. A lot of boys who then grew up among such fathers—i.e., the Baby Boom generation—felt disenfranchised from these distant paternal figures; that's part of where the rage of the Sixties came from.

The rage we see today seems to have many roots. It's almost twenty years since sociologist Lionel Tiger made the argument in his book The Decline of Males *that contraception had played a part in rendering men less useful, less wanted, less needed than they had been before.*[2]

Fr. Arne: At the same time, the idea that fatherhood had become somehow less necessary—common as it is today, on account of massive artificial contraception—was actually ger-

---

[1] Tom Brokaw, *The Greatest Generation* (New York: Random House, 2001).
[2] Lionel Tiger, *The Decline of Males* (New York: Golden Books Publishing Company, 1999).

minating before the Pill came into play, on account of the war. And what is just as concerning now is that the entry of women out of the home and into the paid marketplace may mean that many children today are not only badly fathered, but badly mothered as well.

6

A Few Favorite Things

Philosophers and others have written of the connections between aesthetics and religion, and the ways in which transcendence via beauty lifts human eyes toward God. Readers will be interested to know some of your own go-to favorites. For starters, what's your favorite music?

Fr. Arne: We had a piano growing up, and my mother threatened to get rid of it if we didn't practice. That didn't exactly give me an incentive to practice more! If anything, the opposite. I don't play anything. Since childhood, my instrument of choice has been the CD—and more recently, earbuds.

Favorite composers?

Fr. Arne: When I was younger, Tchaikovsky . . . and of course, Bach, Beethoven, Mozart. Like my taste in books, my musical leanings run toward the classical. As for instruments, the one I most enjoy hearing is cello. I'm a big fan of Yo-Yo Ma.

How about architecture? Did those years in Spain make you a devotee of Spanish Gothic? Or of Antoni Gaudi?

Fr. Arne: Actually, I tend toward Romanesque—simple elegance. Austere elegance is a byword for me in art, as in life. This is not the same as minimalism, but it does mean I shy from the overly ornate. The preference is for classical, neoclassical lines—what's naturally attractive. Art and architecture that's aesthetically balanced draws you peacefully into a space where you can think and work.

Not a fan of Baroque, either?

Fr. Arne: Not really, no. It's cloying after a while. Simplicity in art, as in life, wins for me.

Some harbor a heretical opinion about the Sistine Chapel for that same reason. Michelangelo's figures, especially of women, are superhuman—which is to say, inhuman. Agree?

Fr. Arne: I do.

On a visit to the Frick Museum in New York a few years back, I was feeling overwhelmed by all the artistic ornamentation on display. I found myself gravitating instead to some of Goya's sketches. In just a few lines, he was able to capture a human being. Igor Babailov is able to do that too.[1] It's extraordinary—and at the same time, so very simple.

Following this thread of austere elegance, what are your favorite prayers?

Fr. Arne: The *Magnificat*, Lord's Prayer, *Anima Christi*, and the Rosary.

---

[1]   The portrait artist mentioned in the Introduction.

In truth, I've never been hugely into devotional prayer, though of course I do them every day. My favorite experience of prayer is more conversational, which is something I learned from St. Josemaría—that the whole idea of God the Father is familial. The Christian is invited into the house, and there's a family there. Praying is like talking within a family.

And the saints? In a secularizing time like ours, many people find the idea of saints inexplicable. How do you explain them?

Fr. Arne: They're the close friends of God. It's like having your sidewalk in need of repairs. You're more likely to get it fixed if you have access to someone who is well-connected in the city government.

Which ones do you find especially helpful?

Fr. Arne: St. Thomas Aquinas, St. Josemaría, St. John Paul the Great, Blessed Álvaro del Portillo.[2]

I have a great affection for saintly women. St. Thérèse of Lisieux, with her idea of the Little Way, is one I turn to often.[3]

---

[2] St. Thomas Aquinas (1225–1274) was an Italian Dominican friar and Catholic priest of the thirteenth century and one of the most influential philosophers and theologians in history. St. Josemaría Escrivá (1902–1975), founder of Opus Dei, was canonized in 2002. St. John Paul the Great (1920–2005), aka Pope John Paul II, was born Karol Wojtyla, and was canonized in 2014. Blessed Álvaro del Portillo (1914–1994) was a Roman Catholic bishop who succeeded St. Josemaría Escrivá as the prelate of Opus Dei, serving between 1982 and 1994. He was beatified in 2014.

[3] St. Thérèse of Lisieux (1873–1897) was a French Discalced Carmelite who died of tuberculosis at the age of 24 and became one of the most popular saints of the modern age for her example of simplicity and sanctity. She was canonized in 1925.

St. Martha I have great affection for.[4] Her sister Mary sits at
the Lord's feet, but Martha levels with Him. Martha deals
with Him practically. I have to think that our Lord loved her
frankness.

You see the same practicality in St. Teresa of Ávila, as in
the famous story where she's caught in a brutal downpour on
the way to her convent.[5] Upon falling in the mud, she raises
her eyes to heaven and says, "Lord, if this is how you treat your
friends, it's no wonder you have so few of them." Again, we
see the practicality of women, the meeting of the divine mind
from a position of confidence.

---

[4] The story of Mary and Martha referred to in the text appears in Luke's
   Gospel (Luke 10:38–42).
[5] St. Teresa of Ávila (1515–1582) was a Spanish mystic and Discalced Carmelite whose philosophical writings influenced many inside the Catholic
   Church and out, among them the philosopher René Descartes. She was
   declared the papal honor of Doctor of the Church by Pope Paul VI in 1970.

7

The Phoenix of Hope

Editor's note: On April 4, 2017, Archbishop Charles J. Chaput of Philadelphia visited the Catholic Information Center to discuss his new book, *Strangers in a Strange Land: Living the Catholic Faith in a Post-Christian World*, mentioned in an earlier conversation. Fr. Arne presided over this enthusiastically attended public presentation. The next morning, in the drawing room, we continued to discuss the event.

The Archbishop distinguishes in his opening pages between hope and optimism, as follows: "Christians have many reasons for hope. Optimism is another matter. Optimism assumes that, sooner or later, things will naturally turn out for the better. Hope has no such illusions."

Nonetheless, many believers today are despondent, and think that the best days of Christianity in the West are now behind us.

Fr. Arne: As we've discussed before, the idea of a new Great Awakening has been on my mind for some time. I do think there's one in the offing.

I see it in the Leonine Fellows, for example—in the way that they know they were deprived even by the most prestigious schools of the true glories of Western civilization—and given gruel instead.

And it isn't only a spiritual awakening that's coming. Peter Thiel and I discussed several years ago the impending bursting of the educational balloon. Just think of the attack on Charles Murray at Middlebury College.[1] It's a fiasco. Students leave these schools with no jobs, no intellectual sustenance of worth, and a huge financial debt . . . students are being duped.

There will be a utilitarian reaction to that chasm between what they're promised and what they're actually taught—a market correction, of sorts, in education. But the deeper reaction is more personal. It's about betrayal. Some of these students come to realize that there's a world out there that they never knew existed. They've been purposefully sealed off from it by their teachers and other authorities. That begs for reaction. They've been sold a bill of secular progressive goods!

And I believe the educational awakening and the spiritual awakening will reinforce one another, as a recovery of some of our civilization's substance gets underway.

That's one reason why we see the growth of these counter-institutions like the Leonine Forum—and Thomistic Circles,[2] and the Witherspoon Institute,[3] and like-minded new associa-

---

[1]   On March 2, students disrupted a scheduled talk by social scientist Charles Murray, then surrounded and attacked the car he was riding in with Professor Allison Stanger, the moderator of his speech. She sustained a concussion, and was sent to the hospital with other injuries caused by a student or students twisting her neck.

[2]   Thomistic Circles is a program started by the Thomistic Institute at the Dominican House of Studies in Washington, DC, to bring the Catholic intellectual tradition to campuses. Founded in 2015, it has grown rapidly and now includes chapters on scores of American colleges and universities, as well as in Ireland and England.

[3]   The Witherspoon Institute is an independent research organization in Princeton, NJ, that runs programs and seminars for students in high school

tions that help young people to engage in intellectual dialogue. As we've been talking about elsewhere, discussions are now underway about using the Leonine Forum as a pilot for similar programs, expanding into New York and L.A., for starters.

That's another measure of how hungry people are for transcendence and truth. At least some of the older intellectuals who aren't traditionalists themselves can still understand that appetite.

The lack of transcendence in secularism is its great weakness, alongside its carnality and its hubris of man-as-god. It fails to satisfy what's deepest in us. I share the sense that there's jujitsu afoot—the possibility of revival arising precisely out of these vulnerabilities.

Your mention of Middlebury recalls earlier discussions concerning the filial. There's been a lot of commentary during the past weeks on the violence directed against Charles Murray there and the hospitalization of Professor Allison Stanger. The point's been made repeatedly that this was an assault on free speech. True enough.

But watching the footage, I was struck by something else. Here were scores of young people in the prime of their lives, menacing and even laying violent hands on a man in his seventies, and a middle-aged woman (who, to repeat, ended up in the hospital as a result).

It was so abject, so subversive of any kind of civilization that accords older people respect. And the thought came to mind that today's lack of filial understanding—the flight of the father—also has horrible fallout in another way: it undercuts filial piety, the natural respect of the young for the old, period.

---

and college aimed at studying "the moral foundations of political, philosophical, and social thought."

Fr. Arne: This brings us back to the hunger for the familial in another form: its positive manifestations.

Look at what happened when Pope John Paul II visited Denver for World Youth Day in 1993: massive turnout beyond what anyone foresaw. Or contrast the difference between the Women's March in Washington earlier this year, and any of the annual pro-life marches. The pro-life demonstrations teem with children and teenagers who are buoyant about protecting the human family. The so-called "women's marches" are otherwise: grim. I've often thought that the police who are present at these very different protests must be struck by their diametrically different tones and vibes.

So yes, hope is very much in the offing. We shouldn't fall prey to historicist traps and superstitious beliefs in inevitability. We write history as we go.

I like the image of the phoenix, in that regard.[4] Sometimes it takes a fire to release new life. The very heat of the fire, for instance, releases the seeds from the pine trees.

---

[4] The reference is to "The Phoenix in the Ashes of the Culture War," thecatholicthing.org, April 18, 2017. https://www.thecatholicthing.org/2017/04/18/the-phoenix-in-the-ashes-of-the-culture-wars/

8

What's a Spiritual
Director to Do?

Fr. Arne, I was telling a young woman who's a lifelong Catholic about our continuing conversations. She's dating a man who knows nothing whatever of Christianity except for its role in history books. She asks how you might approach someone in that situation, which as we know is ever more common.

Fr. Arne: As with any spiritual direction, first I want to get the context, the existential background of the person. Where are you from? What's your family situation? Ethnicity, or other significant characteristics? Are you the oldest, or the youngest? How many siblings?

Context is always critical. For example, when I lead retreats, I talk about creation. Our lives have context. We're born in a particular time, to particular families, in particular centuries, etc. It's a treasure trove of wealth and riches.

Spiritual direction is somewhat like being a composer. If you were to have said to Stravinksy, say, "Write me a piece of music," he'd probably have replied that it was impossible, given the open-endedness of the demand. But if instead you asked him to write a piece of music three minutes long, in a given key, and of a particular sort—say, a fugue—suddenly the thing becomes thinkable.

Context is everything, including with human beings.

Usually by the time I've asked my own questions about individual context, the other party is already asking questions of his or her own, about the faith. I suggest, especially to non-believers, that they think first about transcendence. Is there, or is there not, something beyond you that is wonderful and mysterious? Something you may at different times in your life have found intriguing—threatening, even?

I ask them to look back at events in their lives that turned out to be momentous, and that have been written off as chance or luck. For most of us, "chance" or "luck" don't capture the feeling we all know—that at times, what's happened to us is serendipitous, somehow beyond random coincidence.

Very often, I encounter one of the problems you note in *How the West Really Lost God*.[1] If someone's dad was abusive, absent, alcoholic, or otherwise compromised in the paternal role, it's of course commensurately more difficult for that child to understand God as a benevolent, loving father. In that sort of case, which again is common, I might begin with a thought experiment: if there were someone who *had* your best interests at heart, what might that look like? What characteristics might such a father have?

On a related note, how do you approach those people who are not un-Christian, but post-Christian—people raised in some kind of church tradition who have consciously left it?

---

[1] Mary Eberstadt, *How the West Really Lost God: A New Theory of Secularization* (West Conshohocken, PA: Templeton Press, 2013).

Fr. Arne: Here again, so often it's the parental and familial circumstances that influence and even drive that decision. In addition to the obstacles that broken homes create for religious literacy, there may be others as well. Parents, for example, may have found it socially desirable to leave Catholicism for a church with more social cachet, like Episcopalianism.

Another thing that matters is *when* former believers unplug from Christianity. Many young people today have been subjected to banal catechetical programs that have left them with a deformed, bored view of the faith. It can be even more challenging to reach these people than people who have never believed in the first place—because the badly catechized have been misinformed to boot, and remedial education is needed.

Once again, the context is important. You can't love what you don't know. In order to know it, you must be shown something. The great Paul VI was right when he said that "Modern man listens more willingly to witnesses than to teachers, and if he does listen to teachers, it is because they are witnesses."[2]

A few people do read and study their way into the Church—but only a few. Ultimately, most believe because they've been brought in by trusting someone, and they then pass along that same religious fellowship to others.

What about other Christians? How do you approach Protestants?

Fr. Arne: Usually the first things I tell them about are the important items Protestants bring to the table. There are at least four.

Protestantism is usually imbued with a strong sense of Jesus as person; a decent working knowledge of Scripture; a

2   Pope Paul VI, *Address to the Members of the Consilium de Laicis* (October 2, 1974): AAS 66 (1974), 568.

good work ethic (per Max Weber and others); and Protestants generally lack the clerical baggage that many Catholics unfortunately carry with them, i.e., inordinate deference to clergy.

Having acknowledged these truths, I next list what Catholics bring to the table. In general, I make the point that if you read the history of the Church, the idea that it culminates in non-Catholic Christianity doesn't fit the facts. That's because the Protestant churches must always leave something behind, in order to be what they are. The two most important sacraments, for example—Eucharist and Confession—just aren't there in Protestant practice.

For that reason, there's confusion outside Catholic circles—and sometimes also within them—about what Confession really is. I explain that the priest is not doing the absolving himself, but rather that he's the instrument of God, the human vessel through which the divine Father forgives.

Similarly, I explain that the Eucharist isn't just a wafer. It's what Catholics understand to be the Real Presence of the Savior. Apart from a few within the Anglican fold, most Protestants have a very different understanding of these things. In both cases, I explain, what matters is that God is present in these sacraments. No other Christian denomination can offer that.

Your mention of the Real Presence recalls Flannery O'Connor's famous remark, when she retorted to Mary McCarthy as they were sparring about the Eucharist that, "If it's just a piece of bread, then to hell with it."[3]

---

[3] Flannery O'Connor, *The Habit of Being: Letters of Flannery O'Connor* (New York: Farrar, Straus and Giroux, 1988), 125.

I happened to walk through the grounds of the National Cathedral this morning before coming here, and I was struck all over again by the majesty of the Gothic, and how little else man-made on earth compares to the magnificence of these monuments to God. There came a Flannery-style mini-epiphany. I thought, nobody builds this for a piece of bread.

And of course they didn't; when the great Gothic cathedrals were first raised up, the same cathedrals that inspired ours in Washington, no one understood Communion as just a piece of bread, but rather as a house on earth for the sacraments in which God, as you point out, is actually present.

Fr. Arne: Repeatedly, I find as a priest that one reason people come to me who aren't Catholic is exactly that: they hunger for the sacraments, particularly Confession and the Eucharist, sometimes without even knowing it.

Recently a young lawyer with [a prestigious DC firm] was browsing through the CIC bookstore. He wasn't Catholic, but he said that he was there because he really wanted to receive the sacraments. That was an unusual example of someone outside the Church who already knew what he was missing. I put him on the fast track to conversion, and he was received into the Church at Easter. I find with most other people that they know they're missing something; it takes them a little longer, and the right spiritual direction, to figure out what.

9

More Thoughts on the Woman Question

Here's a challenging one for the spiritual director. A friend is an ordained Episcopalian minister. She has a PhD in theology and is a manifestly Christian soul. She seems perturbed by recent developments within the Anglican Communion. I asked her what was keeping her from crossing the Tiber, and she replied: the fact that she couldn't take her clerical status with her and be a priest in the Catholic Church. What would you say to someone in her (admittedly unusual) position?

Fr. Arne: I'd start by having her read Pope John Paul II's *Mulieris Dignitatum*, his 1988 encyclical on the dignity and vocation of women.[1] It's one of the most brilliant Church documents ever penned. He understands the feminine nature as few men can.

Mary was the only human being conceived without sin. No one else in human history even comes close to her moral

---

[1] Apostolic Letter, *Mulieris Dignitatem*, of the Supreme Pontiff John Paul II on the dignity and vocation of women on the occasion of the Marian year, August 15, 1988.

and theological stature. Just look at the Latin describing the situation. There are three kinds of worship: *latria*, or worship given only to the divinity; *dulia*, the honor we give the saints because of their friendship to the Lord; and *hyper-dulia*, a status somewhere between the two. That is Mary.

She is singled out, unique, the only person in the Church to receive that devotion. She's higher than any pope, any priest—any man at all.

And so many of the important undertakings of the ages have been accomplished by women. Think of our own time. Who is really carrying the banner for religious liberty these days? It's the Little Sisters of the Poor.[2] Is that an accident? Or look at Mother Teresa. There was no order to fulfill what she saw as her mission on this earth, caring for the sick and dying, and becoming an ambassador around the world for their cause. She created that role. Women rise up repeatedly to remind the world of what Christianity demands.

Or look at women who aren't known outside their homes and communities. St. Josemaría would say that men have one profession. Women have many. A woman who stays home to raise a family is everything—a chef, a doctor, a psychiatrist, an interior decorator. . . . It's a wonder to behold. And the fruit of all these gifts are the children she raises up.

Anthony Esolen makes this point in his book Out of the Ashes.[3] *He says,* [finding the quote on the phone] "*Consider what a mass of contradictions we are. If a woman arranges flowers for a*

---

2   The Little Sisters of the Poor are an international congregation of Catholic women religious founded in 1839. They live in community with the elderly poor. The Little Sisters became national news following Obamacare's con-traceptive mandate, which tried to force them and other religious groups to provide contraception in violation of their religious beliefs.

3   Esolen, *Out of the Ashes*, 127.

living, she earns our congratulations even if she doesn't do any-thing else. . . . *If a woman cooks fine Italian meals for a living—if her gnocchi, with their wonderful hundreds of calories, are famous all over town—we sing her praises, even if when she gets home she is spent. If a woman plays the violin or gives singing lessons, she can hope to find her name in the newspapers.* . . . *But if a woman, because she is well-versed in all of the household arts, can do all these things and in fact does them for the people she loves and for those whom she welcomes into her home* . . . *we shake our heads and say that she has wasted her talents."*

Fr. Arne: Yes. In *Bleak House,* there was the example of Miss Jellyby, the woman who was so dedicated to social activism—missions and other matters outside her home—that her children were all over the map. There's plenty of that today too.

Humorist P. J. O'Rourke captured a similar thought. He said: "Everyone wants to save the world. No one wants to help Mom with the dishes."

Back to discussion! Do you find young women today are bothered by the same issues that bedeviled many of their mothers—career first, and all that?

Fr. Arne: Absolutely not. It's very much a generational thing.[4]

We know from survey data that women today self-report as being less happy than they used to be. We also know that there's been a marked rise in self-destructive behaviors: alcoholism and opioid addiction being the most measurable.

---

[4]   The unique situation of modern women is taken up in more detail in the sections ahead on "Guidance for Young Professionals," "Simple Rules for Modern Souls," and "Love and Marriage."

The usual answers are proposed to explain such things: income inequality, wage stagnation, and other purported economic factors. But does anybody really dive into a pill bottle over the genie coefficient? The elephant among us, again, seems to be the implosion of the family via divorce, cohabitation, contraception, and the rest of the familiar accompaniments. The pressure on women to be what Ashley McGuire has recently dubbed "failed men" is enormous.[5]

Fr. Arne: Yes, that's the flip side of our earlier reflection on what the filial rupture is accomplishing. We've looked already at what it's done to men. What it's doing to women is just as bad—maybe even worse.

---

[5] Ashley McGuire, *Sex Scandal: The Drive to Abolish Male and Female* (Washington, DC: Regnery, 2017).

10

More Thoughts about
Hope and Love

Fr. Arne, last week after our meeting I attended a conference of philanthropists, many of them ardent Christians, who work to help the poor. Their felt need to find something to believe in was palpable. Here were people wanting only to do good with the resources they have, and as one of them said, almost plaintively, "Just give me something to hope for."

It was striking how the search for leadership and hope seems to have become ubiquitous. Could you meditate for a bit more on hope?

Fr. Arne: St. Thomas Aquinas defines hope as a longing for a future difficult good for which we have an expectation. It's not something entirely in our control. There's a sense of dependency in hope.

You and I have spoken a lot about the budding and established institutions that point toward hope. Robby [George] does the same.[1] There's the Anscombe Society, the Love and

---

[1] Robert P. George is the McCormick Professor of Jurisprudence at Princeton University.

Fidelity Network, and so many others.[2] St. Josemaría liked to call their shared mission "the virtue of holy purity."

The question, of course, is what is love? It's one of those intangibles. You can define it; but once you try to articulate it you've lost its existential quality. You have to experience it to understand it.

One of the great tragedies of our time, and what I see over and over as a priest, is that there are so many people who believe they are unloved, and unlovable. But they're wrong. God makes us always lovable.

In his novel The Power and the Glory, *set in Mexico during the revolutionary era when the Church was persecuted, Graham Greene puts that thought into the mouth of his fallen whiskey priest. He says of God's love: "It set fire to a burning bush in the desert, didn't it, and smashed open graves and set the dead walking in the dark. Oh, a man like me would run a mile to get away if he felt that love around."*

Does humanity turn away from transcendence because we fear what we may be asked in return?

Fr. Arne: All love is sacrificial. There is no love without suffering, not in this world, anyway. One reason humanity flees God, as in the example of the whiskey priest, is that it loses temperance and fortitude, as we discuss elsewhere in these talks.

---

[2] The Anscombe Society is a nonreligious student organization inspired by the example of the influential moral philosopher Elizabeth Anscombe. Dedicated "to affirming the importance of the family, marriage, and a proper understanding of the role of sex and sexuality," and widely seen as an alternative to the hook-up collegiate culture, it has chapters on many American campuses. The Love and Fidelity Network, founded in 2007, brings together hundreds of students across the country for an annual conference organized around similar traditional themes.

Another is that humanity is brash. The very idea of heroism consisting in little things, and that this is the true path to holiness, affronts some. They think it's too much to ask that they persevere day after day in this disciplined way.

A third way of running away from God has its origins in the feeling of unworthiness. The modern mind is captured here by T. S. Eliot: "Do I dare to eat a peach?" There's an uncertainty, a feeling of being unloved, and again, that's one I see afflicting today's men and women all the time.

This idea of fraudulence is one of the most unexpected themes to emerge in our talks, at least on this end. It's a finding that might surprise others too. Your repeated observation that so many people today are afflicted with the feeling that they don't deserve redemption has got to be significant, as is your thought that this anxiety is part of what's driving secularization itself.

Fr. Arne: It's what I hear constantly. Many people today don't feel loved, and they also fear that they're not loveable.

That's why I like to start religious retreats with the Book of Genesis, to rehearse the story of Creation and to emphasize that all of this world—everything in it—is for *us*. God has gone to great lengths to give us a context. To understand that is to see a loving hand in everything around us, to think of love as something other than just an emotive feeling.

Some people think that if only they'd lived in another time—the Middle Ages, the Victorian years—they'd somehow have become more themselves. That's nonsense. What they need to understand is that God has given each of us a specific context: the year we were born, the birth order in our family, the place and moment in history—all of it.

I tell people: Don't run away from the reality in which God has placed you. Its richness is all there for *you*.

One of my favorite stories in the Old Testament is that of David and Absalom. David wasn't flawless. So why does God say that "David is a man who will do my will," given all the sins committed by David?

The answer lies in the end of the story. After Absalom commits his own share of sins, including having himself anointed and sending David on the lam, Absalom is killed . . . and David's response is still that of a loving father: "O my son Absalom! My son, my son Absalom! If only I had died instead of you! O Absalom . . ."[3]

This story gives us a glimpse into the heart of God. David is beloved despite all his sins, and particularly because he responds to his errant son as God responds to us: first and foremost, a loving father.

God never tires of forgiving; we may tire of asking forgiveness. No matter what we've done, He would rather die than have us die.

One has to come to that understanding of God to understand the Catholic faith.

Is it necessary to be a mystic to understand these things?

Fr. Arne: It isn't. I'd be hard pressed to say I've ever had a mystical experience.

That said, there are glimpses we catch that draw us toward transcendence, that knock us out of our comfort zones. True, as the title of Michael Novak's book had it, following Deu-

---

[3]   2 Sam 18:33.

teronomy, *No One Sees God.*[4] But at the same time, there are intimations of the divine that have a buoyancy to them, and change lives.

Do you see a lot of that as a priest?

Fr. Arne: I had three different conversations just yesterday, each about exactly such profound things.

---

[4] Michael Novak, *No One Sees God: The Dark Night of Atheists and Believers* (New York: Doubleday Religion, 2008).

11

Guidance for Young Professionals

Fr. Arne, you've spent many years working with young adults after they've left college and as they embark on careers, including at the CIC, and via the Leonine Forum and other groups. What particular guidance do you suggest for them?

Fr. Arne: I begin with the fact that we live in the most affluent society ever known. Temperance and fortitude may be harder to come by, because abundance brings heightened temptation and distractions. I encourage them to develop intellectual fortitude—to fortify their minds against random, insubstantial, ephemeral influences so rampant in the age of the internet.

I also counsel them in *affective* fortitude, which is a rarer thing; this is the ability to be a master of one's own mind, imagination, and memory, and not unduly influenced by the opinions and affections of others—or lack thereof.

In light of exactly our unparalleled material abundance, what do you counsel them about charity? What are their obligations to the rest of humanity?

Fr. Arne: I begin not with the material or monetary side, but by addressing the most corrosive impediments to charity: anger, vindictiveness, suspicion.

Young professionals, like everyone else, need to understand that they are a tempting target for the devil. *Diabolo* means literally "scatterer," and that is how evil operates: by putting obstacles between individuals and true community.

His first weapon is lust. The sexual appetite is all-powerful, because it engenders a powerful good: the propagation of humanity itself. When the sexual appetite is turned to selfish self-indulgence, it destroys not only individuals, but a whole culture.

When lust doesn't work for the devil, or even if it does, he goes after charity. Once more: suspicion, vindictiveness, anger, and other such feelings are inimical to charity, because they divide people from one another.

In all cases, I encourage spiritual jujitsu. When you begin to feel any of these divisive emotions, be self-aware, and immediately say a prayer for whoever is the object of your anger or resentment. This sets your spiritual house in order, and keeps you closer to community, and less scattered.

So the first line of thought I'd advance about charity is the necessity of getting one's spiritual, interior life framed correctly, the better to give the right sort of material help.

Second, as a practical matter, let's take one that comes up constantly in downtown Washington, DC, and many other cities: the question of what to do for or about the homeless. I counsel people that when they see someone on the street, and know they are going to bypass that person, they should first say a prayer to two guardian angels—their own, and that of the individual on the street.

Second, pray a Hail Mary for that person. These prayers establish that you are in dialogue with and about the human being in the street.

Third, always acknowledge the presence of that man or woman—with a smile, a wave, a "good morning" or "God bless you" or the like—regardless of whether you give them anything. This establishes human connection, which often is a critical part of what the city's homeless men and women are seeking.

Fourth, if you choose to give anything material, I advise food, coffee, a soft drink rather than money. That way you've given something of sustenance, rather than alms that might be used for the person's detriment. Food and drink establish a personal connection as coins do not—and again, personal connection is one of the most vital things that many street people are lacking.

What about tithing? Do you advise it? Do you have a literal guideline in mind?

Fr. Arne: I do advise tithing, and I don't offer anyone a set percentage. Personal circumstances are too variable for that. I approach this area, too, by looking first at the immaterial, and then moving to the material.

There are three levels of tithing. One can give money; one can give time; one can give of one's self. Most often, the difficulty is in that ascending order. Many people, ironically, actually find it easier to write a check than to work in a soup kitchen, or to serve on the board of a charitable institution, or otherwise to give of time or self.

In guiding young professionals, I like to plant the phrase "elegant austerity" as a yardstick for their lives. It's about having what is appropriate for your station in life, appreciating it, and not being led into ever more extravagant temptations.

Is a Lamborghini "bad"? In principle, no. But going into debt in order to buy one means that servicing that debt will displace opportunities for charity. Again, there is no hard-and-fast rule in all this. We're aided in discernment by the fact that when people are being self-indulgent about anything, they usually know it.

What about those who are exceptionally fortunate materially, and who want to put their resources toward charitable works on a larger scale? There's always discussion about whether they should dispose of their assets before dying, or create a family foundation, etc.—about how best to use their wealth for the common good. Any thoughts?

Fr. Arne: One important guideline can be found in the phrase for which Arthur Brooks has become famous: "earned success."[1]

Excepting cases of good self-discipline, which are the exception not the rule, I don't advise leaving sizeable trust funds to children—not unless they can be trusted to be good stewards. Many will simply use the money to finance temptation.

And even if they use their resources only to avoid work, there's a problem in that too: work is enriching. There are

---

[1] See Arthur C. Brooks, *The Road to Freedom* (New York: Basic Books, 2012). In an op-ed about the book published in the *Wall Street Journal* on May 8, 2012, he adds: "Earned success means defining your future as you see fit and achieving that success on the basis of merit and hard work. It allows you to measure your life's 'profit' however you want, be it in money, making beautiful music, or helping people learn English. Earned success is at the root of American exceptionalism."

certain virtues you can only acquire by working. Parents who understandably want to protect their children need neverthe-less to understand that protecting them from work itself is no favor to the child and can be spiritually detrimental.

12

Thoughts about the Environment

Fr. Arne, let's start today with a subject of interest to growing numbers of people inside and outside the Church. Many young adults, unbelievers and believers alike, have come to regard the environment as an area of particular moral concern. Some thinkers, especially within tradition-minded religious circles, are wary of this concern, because they see environmentalism as a de facto substitute for religion, particularly among Millennials.

But let's leave those arguments aside. We can all agree that there's an authentic desire to protect the environment, springing from an equally authentic desire to do good. How do you counsel people to situate this moral concern for the physical world correctly?

Fr. Arne: Let's go back to the Eisenhower Interstate highways. The idea was to build long stretches of highway through pristine territory to aid faster and better driving. This meant the creation of rest stops and signs, etc. I can remember that by the time one reached the five-mile marker, very often you wouldn't need the sign, because so many people were jettisoning trash from their cars. The bucolic highway was becoming a bicoastal garbage dump.

In a parallel way, the Charles River in the 1960s, when I was living in Cambridge, Massachusetts, was so toxic that we joked about needing tetanus shots if we'd been splashed with its water.

That was then. As it turned out, many people reacted against this defacing of nature. They decided to do something about the decay and debris rather than just accepting it as fact. The same happened later with air pollution and smoking. Roads, national parks, and air all were the better for it, as were people.

Pope Benedict makes an interesting parallel in this regard: that as we look at concern for the toxicity of the physical environment, we need also to be concerned about the toxicity of the moral environment.[1]

What's wonderful about that formulation is its expansiveness, its repudiation of zero-sum thinking. Pope Benedict is saying that concern about A needn't—and shouldn't—drive out concern about B. The search for right living isn't a zero-sum game.

On a similar point, concern for unborn human life needn't exist apart from the concern for animal welfare; if anything, the two are more closely aligned, including in Church teaching, than is commonly understood.

Concern for what's right doesn't boil down to a competition of warring moral factions—that's a point that really resonates with younger people, especially, once they know that's what the Church is about.

---

[1]   Pope Benedict XVI, *Address of His Holiness Benedict XVI to Students Participating in a Meeting Promoted by the 'Sister Nature' Foundation*, November 28, 2011.

Fr. Arne: Yes. That's why we include talks about the pro-animal, pro-life connection for members of the Leonine Forum. They're always interested in that moral synergy.

Of course, there are prudential judgments involved in environmentalism. Concern alone doesn't answer the question of science, for example; one has to use one's reason in assessing the differing claims of scientists, for example, with regard to global warming. Within the community of those who study it, that phenomenon is said to differ wildly depending on which scholar is advancing which particular thesis.

The irony of environmentalism having become big business, including big government business—cap and trade, subsidization of certain companies at the expense of others—suggests intellectual cautiousness about precisely *what* one believes; there are too many examples already of how ideology in these matters can be used as a bludgeon which then turns into a financial windfall for savvy big-government entrepreneurs.

This seems to be a case in which the principle of subsidiarity could help us to make useful distinctions.[2]

Fr. Arne: The trouble with environmentalism as some now construe it is that if you say the problem is "carbon emission" or "the ozone layer" or related abstractions, individuals find that overwhelming. That's why people become resigned to having government discharge the moral obligation, or try to—because it looks like only a big organization can solve such a big problem.

---

[2] The concept of "subsidiarity" originates from Catholic social teaching and refers to the organizing principle that decisions are best handled by the smallest, nearest, least-centralized authority.

And that's precisely what sets the stage for potential malfeasance: the fact that individuals have effectively outsourced their concern to a faceless entity over which they exercise little oversight. That's what's meant by violating the principle of subsidiarity. Picking up trash from the road you're driving on is the better way.

Back to what Pope Benedict observed about the parallels between the moral and physical worlds: part of why so many outside the Church fail to understand the richness of Christian teaching is that they've been sold a bill of goods about such things. They're told, for example, that the pro-life movement only cares for the fetus, and not to what happens for the rest of a human being's life.

People who believe that have been bamboozled. No one has done more than the Church to care for vulnerable women and children. The Church invented hospitals. The Church in America has had the best adoption agencies connecting unloved children with loving families. The Church abounds with charities designed to help the infirm, the marginalized, the outcasts, the people whom everyone else has thrown away—look again at the Little Sisters of the Poor, whose mission is to care for and live as family with dying people whom no one else wants. All that is just a beginning.

Ever since the Enlightenment, prejudices against Christianity have been assembled and presented as fact to an unsuspecting world that doesn't know the Church, or the truth—small-t, or capital-T.

Rodney Stark's recent book *Bearing False Witness*, about the deliberate, usually self-interested development over centuries of misrepresentations concerning the Church, is such an excellent corrective.[3] He's not a Catholic. He's a historian who doesn't want people to learn false history.

It's wonderful to think that the centuries-long public relations campaigns against Christianity may finally be getting called out. It's one more reason for hope in the future.

[3] Rodney Stark, *Bearing False Witness: Debunking Centuries of Anti-Catholic History* (West Conshohocken, PA: Templeton Press, 2016).

13

Simple Rules for
Modern Souls

Fr. Arne, you are known and treasured for your spiritual direction. Bearing in mind secular and non-Catholic readers, especially, could you explain what spiritual direction is?

Fr. Arne: Spiritual direction is all about seeing life from another person's point of view. That's why, when I meet someone for direction for the first time, I ask a lot of questions—their biography, spiritual life, etc. Obviously, it takes time for this to work. Behind the scenes, I pray for them.

Spiritual direction is like watering and fertilizing. Both are exogenous to the plant itself; but without them, it can't grow.

What do you tell people who are thinking about spiritual direction for the first time?

Fr. Arne: That it's like being a coach, a personal trainer—only for the soul. People can relate to that.

Should every Catholic have a spiritual director?

Fr. Arne: If they're serious about growing in their faith, yes. We're called to be saints. That doesn't happen without work. Some investment has to be made in the project.

What have you learned from guiding all these people so intensely, over so much time?

Fr. Arne: We all have a hesitancy to let ourselves be known. We all have an opaque side that we don't want anyone else to see. Everyone is put together in this same way. When people hold back, it's because they don't yet understand that being known is the opposite of what they fear. It's liberating.

One of my many discoveries about spiritual direction in high-powered Washington, DC, is how common it is for people who are in fact very capable to fear that they'll be exposed as frauds. This is based, again, on a fear of not being loved. The twin fear is not being love-*able*—and this, as we've discussed before, goes back to ruptured filiation.

What's the starter kit for spiritual direction?

Fr. Arne: I suggest four pillars that people should touch daily.

First, morning prayer on the knees. Use "Abba"—talk to God as Father. Also pray to your guardian angel. These prayers don't have to take long. But they're important, because we need daily reminders that we aren't alone out there.

The spiritual bookend to morning prayer is prayer at the end of the day. I recommend three Hail Mary's—for purity: purity of heart, purity of mind.

Third, sometime during the first two hours of your waking day, have fifteen minutes of conversational prayer with Our Lord. Talk. Listen. You have to work at this.

People of the intellectual bent tend to think that if a thought comes to them while they're in prayer, it's just their imagination. They need to cede control. It's about being able to let go of your illusions of control and let God in. This is the hardest part of these four pillars.

Finally, at the end of the day, take three or four minutes to examine your conscience. Ask yourself: Lord, what did we accomplish from the morning prayer?

I find that sloth is an enormous impediment for so many. St. Josemaría said: Sloth is the first battlefront. Greed, sensuality, attachment to material things, indifference, anger—all of these come later.

Everyone should practice spiritual jujitsu. Turn your resentment against another into a Hail Mary said on behalf of that person. Guardian angels are a big help with that. So is daily Mass, for those who can make it.

14

John Henry Newman and Josemaría Escrivá, Con't.

Editor's note: The following conversation, on June 1, 2017, was especially memorable, both because of the glorious setting, and because Fr. Arne was so energetic that we spoke that morning for over two hours. Following several days of rain, Washington, DC, was finally allowed a day of brilliant spring weather. We sat outside in the garden of his residence, where hydrangeas and primroses were in bloom, chipmunks and cardinals made regular appearances, and a bubbling fountain neutralized the sound of traffic on the other side of the wall.

We seem to have been given more time than we thought we'd have when we started these conversations![1] So let's make the most of it.
I'd like to go back and ask you to describe your dissertation on John Henry Newman in a little more detail. For readers who may not have heard of him, this Anglican priest who converted to Catholicism and later became a cardinal was one of the most intel-

---

[1] Medical expectations were that Fr. Arne would die shortly after being sent home on hospice care. This conversation took place almost four months later.

lectually influential churchmen of the nineteenth century.[2] *He's a fascinating example of the power of revival, including in moments when the Church appears to many to be in irreparable decline. As such, he's obviously a potent exemplar in a secularizing time. What was your particular focus in making him the object of your doctorate?*

Fr. Arne: The dissertation was called "John Henry Newman and the Force of History." I believe there's a copy in the archives at Pamplona, Spain, University of Navarre. It runs to six hundred pages and covers two volumes.

Newman began his philosophical life with Calvinism. His problems with Catholicism were the usual Protestant objections, including to the role of Mary and the pope. He read the fathers of the Church in Greek and Latin, and in the late 1820s started a book on the Arian heresy.[3] When he finished, he went to Rome and met Cardinal Henry Edward Manning and left with the idea that he had work to do in England. On his return he started what became known as the Oxford Movement, a collection of High Church members of the Church of England which eventually developed into Anglo-Catholicism—an attempt to bring what they saw as the secularizing Church of England more in line with its heritage, including the doctrines of the early Church fathers and that of apostolic order.

Newman sought a *via media*—a path between Anglicanism and Roman Catholicism; and he wanted to re-situate the

---

[2] Beatified in 2010, Newman became a major instrument of the conversion of many others via his leadership of the Oxford Movement and his extraordinary literary and philosophical *oeuvre*.

[3] John Henry Newman, *The Arians of the Fourth Century: Their Doctrine, Temper, and Conduct, Chiefly as Exhibited in the Councils of the Church, between AD 325 & AD 381*, first published by Rivington in 1833.

COE [Church of England] along those lines. Then a series of events too many to detail here convinced him that the Church of England had become primarily political and expedient. Newman concluded that the *via media* didn't exist. In the course of a decade, he came to see that what he thought he'd gone to England to create could never become a reality.

Still, many people continued to look up to him as a leader. He began writing the *Essay on the Development of Christian Doctrine*, intending to explain his reasons for entering the Roman Catholic Church.[4] He had studied Vincent of Lerins, who wrote his *Communitorium* in the early fifth century, which argued there was an organic continuum of doctrinal development.[5] Newman applied that insight to doctrine, and came up with a series of tests or rules for what is and isn't a valid development in doctrine.

For all that, what interested me most was something else: what Newman was really writing in his profoundly influential essay was his own spiritual autobiography.

Would you call that a Straussian reading?[6]

---

4   John Henry Cardinal Newman, *An Essay on Development of Christian Doctrine*, first published in 1888; available in paperback with Foreword by Ian Ker (South Bend IN: Notre Dame Press [Notre Dame Series in the Great Books, No. 4], 1994).

5   St. Vincent of Lerins, *The Commonitory of St. Vincent of Lerins*, excerpted from A Select Library of the Nicene and Post-Nicene Fathers, ed. Philip Schaff, vol. 11, *Sulpitius Severus, Vincent of Lerins, John Cassian* (Veritatis Splendor, 2012; repr. Buffalo, NY: Christian Literature Co., 1886).

6   The reference is to political philosopher Leo Strauss, who argued that serious writers across history employ layered or multiple meanings in their work, with "exoteric" language intended for the public, and "esoteric" or secret teaching that only knowledgeable readers can discern.

Fr. Arne: Let me think about that. I wasn't familiar with Strauss when I wrote it, though we may have been on similar tracks.

My thesis is about how external events in the COE, and God working providentially and serendipitously in Newman's life, proved more powerful than anything that this prodigious intellect was reading. It's about the effort to integrate what's revealed in Scripture and held as dogma with the reality of Providence.

These days, I have even more reason to see God's beneficence working itself out every day. That's what I was pursuing with the thesis on Newman—the way God gently but powerfully moves the lives of individuals.

You're a man of the book—or many books, all those at the CIC, all those in your mind; you live and breathe words, arguments, ideas. Yet from early on, you're at least as interested in the subrational, supernatural forces at work in what people believe and do.

Fr. Arne: Yes. I wanted others to understand the deeper why of what Newman was doing.

We've spoken earlier about one of the other spiritual figures to have influenced you most—St. Josemaría Escrivá, founder of Opus Dei and one of the most important religious figures of the century after Newman. You knew him personally, as discussed earlier, and he obviously had a momentous role in your formation. Would you like to share some more thoughts about your experience of him?

Fr. Arne: Everyone wanted to know the same thing when he was canonized. Everyone asked the same question of me: Did you ever think you'd known a saint? Because many who knew him thought they had.

Did I know I was with a saint? My take is a little different. To be sure, I wasn't present at liturgical moments with him, meaning, on the altar together. I do know that people who served Mass alongside him felt deeply moved by his person at those times. When I think of him, I think first of his great sense of humor. That may seem odd. If you read his best-known book, *The Way*, you can see it's not a knee-slapper—more like a face-slapper.[7] Yet his humor was ever present. He could be earthy, but never went over the line. He laughed deeply.

Of course, capturing that was made harder by his self-imposed guideline of "doing and disappearing." Later in his life, when followers and others wanted to film his many get-togethers, he resisted. In fall 1972 he spent two months going from Pamplona to other points in Spain to Portugal, teaching and meeting and catechizing.

Finally, somewhere during that trip, an argument managed to convince him to allow cameras. It was: "Look Father, if we don't do this, future generations will either think we didn't love you—or that we're stupid. It won't bother us to be thought stupid. But to have them think we didn't love you would be too much to bear."

That's what finally broke the wall and allowed for recordings.

So did you feel as if you'd known a saint after all?

Fr. Arne: At the time, I didn't know what it was like to be around a saint. We have a stereotype, sometimes a caricature,

---

[7]   St. Josemaría Escrivá, *The Way* (Strongsville, OH: Scepter, 1992).

of saints—that they're pious, devout, prone to great gestures
of historical importance.

He was pastoral. He gave a great deal of importance to the
little things. He didn't prize luxury or lavishness, but instead
a sense of the *appropriate*. The Opus Dei centers around the
world convey that sensibility and that spirituality. They're
meant to feel like family homes, familial, warm—neither
overly austere nor overly indulgent.

Not exactly Villa D'Este?[8]

Fr. Arne: Ha! Sometimes that faithfulness to the idea of
home backfires in funny ways. In California, we ran a center
for teenage boys from bad neighborhoods. I remember that
once a socialite, a benefactor, came around to see the place and
seemed almost disappointed; she was expecting to see graffiti
on the walls and garbage in the corners. But instead it was just
one more Opus Dei center dedicated to being a home.

St. Josemaría would point to the Holy Family as the model
of family life. They weren't rich, obviously. But they also weren't
destitute. They had what they needed, like tools, a dwelling,
food, maybe a donkey. The way to be free of materialism is to
have what you need, what's appropriate to you.

Here are a couple of other examples of his thinking. The
central headquarters of Opus Dei is an upscale area just north
of Villa Borghese in Rome, formerly the Hungarian embassy
there. One day he entered and saw that the carpet in the foyer
had been moved around by cleaners, and that the chairs and
table on it were in the wrong places. He asked a student to

---

[8] The opulent sixteenth-century villa in Tivoli, near Rome, commissioned
by Cardinal Ippolito II d'Este and famous for its elaborate and luxurious
gardens, apartments, and fountains.

help him, and they spent a few minutes straightening things and rearranging the furniture. St. Josemaría then said to the student: "Do that same work saying, 'God, this is for you.' Now *that* is Opus Dei."

On another occasion, a student who'd been living in the residence for two years mentioned in passing that a couple of things in his room had been broken the whole time. St. Josemaría commented, "That son of mine. He's been here for two years and hasn't learned a thing." It was hyperbole, of course, but it helped to get the lesson across: work matters. The small things matter.

Again, when most of us think of sanctity, we think of the extraordinary, the dramatic; and that was foreign to his understanding that everyone is called to holiness, that sanctity resides in the ordinary realities of daily life.

And that, I did see in him.

His memory for other people was incredible. He'd recall nicknames, favorite snacks, other details of people he hadn't seen in many years. Another salient point: even when he corrected people, he never gave them the sense that he was keeping track, keeping score, keeping his eyes on them. Nor was his affection ever mitigated by others transgressing.

Javier Eccheveria, successor to Blessed Álvaro, came to Rome at seventeen or eighteen and joined Opus Dei. At the time, the building was being rearranged. St. Josemaría gave instructions to move some of his books and papers, and not to disturb them otherwise. Eccheveria happened to see a stack of calling cards with the priest's name on them, and took one as a souvenir. St. Josemaría gave him a strong reprimand. He said, "If you don't do what I say, then how can I trust you?"

But it wasn't strike one. A week later, he made Eccheveria his personal secretary, at which point of course Eccheveria could have gone through anything he liked. The point was obedience, including in small things.

That story makes a point about transparency. As you say, the secretary was free to see whatever he chose. Allowing access like that isn't the signature of someone with something to hide. This, again, goes to one of our earlier conversations about the gap that exists between the reality of Opus Dei on the one hand, and its bizarre reputation, particularly among secular people, on the other. How did Opus Dei get a reputation for exactly the opposite of transparency—for secrecy and skullduggery?

Fr. Arne: Ironically, I think it is partly derived from the modesty of St. Josemaría himself.

He didn't even want a name for this organization—not one with his own name in it, that is. He didn't want anything distinctive, for instance, a habit, or other accoutrement worn by religious—not even a lapel pin. His saying, again, was "do and disappear." The incorrect inference made by some seems to have been that if they weren't standing out, then members of Opus Dei must have something to hide.

This brings us to a difficult question that everyone has had to think about since 2002—the year when the Catholic priest sex scandals became what George Weigel has called "the long Lent." Many would say that nothing has done more to harm the contemporary Church than the scandals. Yet Opus Dei wasn't much discussed in the context of those events—meaning, offenders didn't seem to be flourishing there, as opposed to elsewhere. Is that an accurate summary of the record?

Fr. Arne: Any priest who says Mass every day, or the Liturgy of the Hours, or any of the rest of the discipline embraced within Opus Dei, isn't fertile territory for the evil seeds that led to the scandals.

Those seeds were planted during the 1960s and 1970s under quite the opposite circumstances, at a time when many within religious orders, especially, ceased living *as* religious. These were priests and nuns who had decided to live without their habits, or without community, at times even in their own apartments. Meanwhile, their spiritual lives were being further undermined by psychiatrists telling them various falsehoods— for example, that religion itself was repressive, and that they should reject its supposed repression and live "freely"; or that men with a sexual appetite for the young could be reined in easily, "treated" for a year or two, and sent back.

It was a time of great confusion, and people swept up in that confusion, and drawn to that confusion, ended up creating the scandals.

You seem to be drawing a line straight from the aftermath of Vatican II to the scandals.

Fr. Arne: Not a line—a bell curve. If you look at the data about the cases, as the Columbia University study did, that's what you find: the offenses for the most part build up through the seventies and into the eighties, and then start trending downward.[9]

---

[9] The reference is to "The Causes and Context of Sexual Abuse of Minors by Catholic Priests in the United States, 1950–2010: A Report Presented to the United States Conference of Catholic Bishops by the John Jay College Research Team," John Jay College of Criminal Justice, 2004, available from http://www.bishop-accountability.org/reports/2011_05_18_John_Jay_Causes_and_Context_Report.pdf.

Widespread moral collusion between clergy and laity seems to have been another sine qua non *of the scandals. There was obviously an understanding of sorts in the years after the Council according to which priests wouldn't bother the laity about contraception, and in return the laity would turn a blind eye to whatever Father was up to after hours. Do you think St. Josemaría, who lived into the seventies, anticipated any of that coming disaster?*

Fr. Arne: He had an inkling that something cataclysmic was coming. Certainly, he was deeply pained about several developments following Vatican II.

One was the disrespect for the Eucharist that developed out of seemingly innocuous attempts to make the Mass into something more like a fraternal meal—like using homemade bread and improvising other elements in the alleged effort to make it "more like the Last Supper." I remember telling someone embarked on such an effort that if they really wanted to be true to the event, they'd have to take the guy who made the dinner outside and nail him to a tree afterwards. I guess no one wanted to be *that* authentic.

St. Josemaría was similarly distressed about efforts to do away with Eucharistic devotion, and to downplaying devotion to Mary and the saints. It's true that sometimes devotion to the saints, especially, can be taken too far; he was certainly aware of that in Spain. But the overall effect of all these diminutions was a lowering of respect for the Church and its sacraments.

Particularly dangerous, he thought, was the undermining of both the Eucharist and Confession—the mainstays of any Catholic.

Even so, throughout all the concerns his watchword was the one I mentioned earlier: "I will obey."

15

Joys and Challenges
of Being a Priest

Fr. Arne, you've been a priest for forty-three years. What have been your greatest joys and greatest challenges?

Fr. Arne: The greatest joy is seeing grace actually work in people. The optic that a priest has is to see grace operate in the life of another soul in a way that the individual himself may be too close to see. It's all very real. This is something I've been particularly fortunate to see often during my years here in Washington.

I have a slight regret about my years in California, only because I was a great outdoorsman, athletic, and loved sports. Hiking, skiing, tennis were all constants of the California life, and sometimes I wish I'd read a little more during that time. Of course I read—just not as much as I probably should have. I also organized various seminars aimed mainly at people breathing in the toxic fumes of relativism, including one called Big Pictures for Dummies.

The serious point is that even now, and like many of us, I have to fight the tendency to turn immediately toward action and projects. It's always been easy for me to fall into that administrative mode. I have to ask, "Lord, don't let me flee from you."

That's not the same kind of fleeing that Graham Greene's whiskey priest wants, of course. But it's still a move away from prayer and God, or can be.

The CIC is well-known for the conversions that happen inside its walls, from congressmen and other machers *to many other people whose names will never be known. We know that according to Catholic teaching, you aren't exactly "responsible" for these entries into the Church. But if we say instead that you've been the instrument of conversion, how many might you estimate you've presided over?*

Fr. Arne: I would always say we have to give some credit to the Holy Spirit! Conversion is one more working out of God's Providence—of giving people what they truly need. Conversion happens all the time and, from the priest's perspective, it's just about being available.

Especially in these days of my decline, I get feedback from many who did convert, expressing gratitude for my instrumentality. I have to admit that I didn't always see the depth of the impact, didn't see some of them growing as profoundly as they did. It's a new way of viewing grace in retrospect.

What about challenges? Many people might guess that the life of a Catholic priest can be lonely. Has that ever been a problem?

Fr. Arne: No, I'm a sanguine person. I love that John Henry Newman's quoting of Cicero, "*Nunquam minus solus quam cum solus*"—never less lonely than when alone. Precisely because I'm a people person, and have lived surrounded with so many others, being alone with our Lord was always something I treasured.

There are several emotions—loneliness, depression, and melancholy—that I've seen a lot of in others, but never experienced myself. It's made me work harder to empathize with people in the throes of those feelings, because I never reached those depths of darkness.

16

Addiction, Depression, and the Modern Mind

Here's another question of interest beyond the Church. Given all your experience of people and of spiritual direction, what do you make of that very modern malady, depression? It seems fair to guess that melancholy we've always had with us. But depression as a clinical phenomenon is so widespread, at least in affluent circles of the West, that it seems as if it must have causal roots in modernity somewhere. Any thoughts on that?

Fr. Arne: Very much so.

We can begin on the surface: the physical/physiological side. I'm persuaded that environmental toxins can be part of that picture. There are empirical realities that might nudge people toward depression.

But of course more important is the isolation of our society—the atomization of the world that we keep returning to in conversation. Many people have no antidote to depression in the form of a caring network, especially the family. Add to that the fact that so many are also trying to live without God. These losses add up to a sense of hopelessness.

Another factor is that we look to technology as a cure for suffering. I have in mind a young man I know, bright and secure in his faith, but hard-driving like so many we know in DC. He suffered from depression and was seeing me for months before he saw a doctor. Ultimately, he was diagnosed as bipolar and treated.

The point is that the story needn't and shouldn't end there, with a technical fix. God isn't absent in this situation. I told him that this affliction is a treasure for him to administer. Having gone through this suffering puts him in a position to help others who suffer similarly. It's like my cancer. It's not to be shunned. It's to be put to the service of others.

Somewhere, there's a line to be drawn between what's medically or empirically explicable, and what's of supernatural origin on the other side. How does one draw it?

Fr. Arne: Part of the humility of being a priest is understanding that we can't understand every problem.

The Italians have a saying: *"il dolce far niente"*: the sweet do nothing. And another: *"Quando il corpo sta bene l'anima balla,"* which means, when the body is sound, the soul dances.

When the body isn't functioning, the soul suffers too. St. Thomas Aquinas points out that there's a minimum of what's needed in order to have the soul in good working order. One needs not to be in extremis. The same thought is behind the Jesuits' embrace of Juvenal's phrase, *Mens sana in copore sano*— sound mind, sound body. Pastors must always treat the whole person.

What about another signal problem of the age—addiction? We read every day about the explosion of opioid addiction, and we're already addicted to so many other toxins, too. Where does addiction come from, and what do you tell people to do about it?

Fr. Arne: Substance abuse is a trouble I see but less than other priests do, because the people who tend to cluster around places like the CIC generally function with a high degree of professionalism. Still, it's there nonetheless.

Addiction to anything springs from the lack of the virtue of temperance. As we've also discussed elsewhere, temperance is harder to come by in our society on account of its affluence. We live in a world where even the poorest still live better, at least as measured by access to comfort and pleasure, than any monarch of the thirteenth century. The opportunities for escape are abundant for all.

What I counsel in cases of addiction depends on the age of the person, among other factors. Say it's someone in high school, smoking marijuana. In such an instance, there's usually a softness, an unwillingness to push themselves. But the problem hasn't yet gone terribly deep.

I tell people that reality is too interesting to want to escape. Escape via chemicals doesn't take anyone to a compelling place. You can't flee to anything more exciting, mysterious, and fascinating than reality itself.

Pornography addiction is also rampant, as we've mentioned. In such cases, I recommend the work of a cognitive therapist (and Opus Dei member) Kevin Majeres of Harvard.[1] His work is summarized by his website, *Purity is Possible.* He works to make people aware of the stressors that lead to addictive actions. Anger, anxiety, and sleep deprivation are all

---

[1]   Kevin Majeres, M.D, is a psychiatrist in Cambridge, MA. The website referenced is www.purityispossible.com.

stressors leading to sexual release and drinking too much. The others are loneliness and boredom.

I tell people to think of themselves as battlefield commanders. They need to go on offense against these stressors. When it's a code red situation on the battlefield, an officer doesn't just sit there. Neither should they.

The devil prefers not to be noticed—to stay hidden. I was just talking yesterday with someone about this metaphor. It's exactly like the 1980s, when the Mafia was pretending not to exist, and dispatched a lawyer for a mob boss to Congress to claim that there was no Mafia. The devil is the same. It's in the interest of evil to have the world deny its existence.

This hiddenness means that evil operates incrementally. For that reason, it can't be eradicated in one fell swoop. You have to walk it down the stairs and show it the door and then lock it out.

With young priests, I always tell them: you're public enemy number one for the devil. If you're a force for the good, you're definitely on his radar screen.

Because of original sin, we all try to escape from God. It needn't be in the way of Francis Thompson fleeing "The Hound of Heaven."[2] Flight takes different forms.

Benedict has described this in a way that no other modern mind has equaled, I believe. Here is his capturing of the modern mind in a 2005 homily on the occasion of the Feast of the Immaculate Conception [searches phone]:

> The human being lives in the suspicion that God's love creates a dependence and that he must rid himself of this dependency if he is to be fully himself. Man does

---

[2]   The reference is to a poem by Francis Thompson, available from www. poemhunter.com.

not want to receive his existence and the fullness of his life from God.

He himself wants to obtain from the tree of knowledge the power to shape the world, to make himself a god, raising himself to God's level, and to overcome death and darkness with his own efforts. He does not want to rely on love that to him seems untrustworthy; he relies solely on his own knowledge since it confers power upon him. Rather than on love, he sets his sights on power, with which he desires to take his own life autonomously in hand. And in doing so, he trusts in deceit rather than in truth and thereby sinks with his life into emptiness, into death.

. . . We have a lurking suspicion that a person who does not sin must really be basically boring and that something is missing from his life: the dramatic dimension of being autonomous; that the freedom to say no, to descend into the shadows of sin and to want to do things on one's own is part of being truly human; that only then can we make the most of all the vastness and depth of our being men and women, of being truly ourselves; that we should put this freedom to the test, even in opposition to God, in order to become, in reality, fully ourselves. In a word, we think that evil is basically good, we think that we need it, at least a little, in order to experience the fullness of being.[3]

---

[3]   Homily of his Holiness Benedict XVI, Solemnity of the Immaculate Conception of the Blessed Virgin Mary, December 8, 2005, available from http://w2.vatican.va/content/benedict-xvi/en/homilies/2005/documents/hf_ben-xvi_hom_20051208_anniv-vat-council.html.

17

Love and Marriage

I've been thinking of a title for our book. How about The Last Homily—*thoughts?*

Fr. Arne: [pauses and nods] I like it. It's like Fr. [James V.] Schall's lecture that he gave on retiring from Georgetown, where he talked about how education is all about friendship.[1] It's good.

Keeping in mind the desire that this book might help and inspire others, it would be wonderful to hear your thoughts on an area of great concern to most people—romance and marriage. When couples come to you, what do you advise?

Fr. Arne: I don't do "marriage prep" per se, and rarely see engaged couples for spiritual direction. Usually, if one is seeing me for spiritual direction, the other wants to see someone else.

---

[1] Fr. James V. Schall, "The Final Gladness," last lecture at Georgetown University, December 14, 2012, available from https://www.youtube.com/watch?v=xN1rFyYbKak.

Is that a have-to?

Fr. Arne: No, but it's most people's choice. That said, if a couple is engaged, I point them toward the marriage prep programs that are better done in a parish, with older couples who can work with them. I think it's very important to have that mentoring. Most of the work I do is with couples who are encountering difficulties in their marriage.

What about discernment—people who are trying to figure out whether to get married in the first place?

Fr. Arne: Now that's a question about vocation, which has two dimensions. One is supernatural: Does God want me to be married? Or to become a member of a religious order? Is my vocation apostolic celibacy? These are questions we all ask— or should.

The first thing I try to do with people who are attempting to discern their vocation is to disabuse them of the notion that God has written in stone what they're supposed to do. They sense, and often wish, that there's some hidden architectural plan out there for them to uncover. But the truth is that there are lots of possibilities.

Let's start with prayer life. The word "vocation" means *call.* The great majority of people are called to marriage. If God wants you to do something else, like become a priest, there are items he'll place in your path—a person, a book, an idea. If you pray and the idea of religious life keeps coming to mind in prayer, that's a sign that you need to explore the thought.

Being called to religious life, for most, involves a degree of *contemptus mundi*, or the notion that the world is a dangerous, damaged place, and that one's personal holiness will require living in a community of the like-minded. Other people are immune to that thought. Generally, if someone loves living in the world, loves working in it, and loves getting their hands dirty, these are all signs that the religious life isn't one's calling. I was very moved by something a young priest once said at a retreat for people contemplating religious life: "Don't think God is going to force you to do this. He loves you far too much simply to take away your freedom." Vocation is a gradual process that evolves as matters are clarified. God doesn't depend on your becoming a doctor, or a lawyer, or other particulars.

Now back to the question of counseling people who are contemplating marriage. For both men and women, I advise for starters that they ask themselves two questions. First, do I see myself spending my life with this individual? And second, do I see this as a lifetime friendship, one in which the person will still be a mystery and able to surprise me?

That's the beginning. For the man, I then also ask: do you see her as the mother of your children? Is she someone who seems open to the dependency and neediness of others?

For the woman, there's a parallel question. Do you see him as the father of your children? Is he someone able to support and be involved in their lives and mine? The flip side is, is he a workaholic? Someone who can't hold a steady job is obviously worth pausing over; but so too is a man whose whole life is work.

Recently, it emerged that a certain nationally known politician follows certain rules in his social life, like not drinking or dining alone with any woman who isn't his wife. Polite society got a good laugh out of that maxim, which many people would judge archaic.

Yet we can easily think of marriages that might have been saved if rules like his had been adopted early on. Everybody knows that one of the fastest ways to torpedo a marriage is through what's called "workplace attractions." Do you address that pitfall with people?

Fr. Arne: That politician's rule is good advice—and a good start. I'd add to it as follows.

I see people fall head over heels in love with someone other than their spouses, all the time—typically men; less often, women. I've worked to help get them out of it. That can take a long time. It's hard work, reorienting the human heart, but it can be done. How much better and easier, though, not to reach that point in the first place.

Again, people need to understand that the devil is alive and active, and there's nothing he likes better than shattering a marriage. Several simple rules help to guard against marital disaster. When travelling with a member of the opposite sex who isn't your spouse, opt for separate flights and separate hotels, insofar as it's possible. That's *prima facie* for appearances' sake, but it's also preventive prudence. If asked to explain, one can always say, "Let's be professional about this."

I also advise that if alcohol is involved, especially at business gatherings in the evening, where it tends to flow liberally because a deal may be at stake, then at a minimum, alternate any alcoholic drink with a nonalcoholic one. I give that same advice to single women, for obvious reasons. So many times during my priesthood, I've counseled guys who rue what they did the night before when they were tired and had too many drinks. Some even end up throwing their careers away because of it. A few preventive rules can amount to powerful protection.

Several years ago, the Witherspoon Institute in Princeton staged a weekend conference on the social costs of pornography.[2] *Doctors, therapists, and former addicts were among those testifying to the devastation brought on in their own lives and the lives of others by what are said to be "just pictures." To sound just one empirical note, pornography use/addiction is a rising factor in divorces and broken homes, as lawyers involved in family court have testified.*

One point made repeatedly was the temptation facing the solo business traveler at the end of the day, including via the omnipresence of smut on televisions and laptops. Do you advise guidelines about that, too?

Fr. Arne: Oh, yes.

First, I tell men that when they check in at the hotel itself, to ask at the desk to have any adult content blocked on the television. If the employee says that isn't possible, then tell them that the next time around you'll look for another hotel. You want to send the message that you want no part, no participation in this stuff.

If the hotel really can't block the channels, then I advise that when the traveler gets to his room, he should take the batteries out of the remote, or unplug the cable, right away. He should also bring along a picture of his wife, or wife and family, or a card with Our Lady on it—something small and discreet that can be propped up against the TV screen. It's amazing how far measures like that will go to keep people safe.

And I counsel them further to go to sleep early and to wake up early—to keep matters professional, to have an endpoint in mind for the trip. So often, trouble comes when it's late at

---

[2] James L. Stoner, Jr., *The Social Costs of Pornography: A Collection of Papers*, ed. Donna M. Hughes (Princeton, NJ: Witherspoon Institute, 2010).

night and tired men are randomly flipping around channels. Boredom and loneliness, as mentioned before, are code red situations. People need to be on guard and take positive action.

We've talked in detail, including here, about challenges that resonate with many men. What about women? Which are the specific temptations and challenges these days of what used to be called the fair sex?

Fr. Arne: The answer to that one begins in Genesis 3:16. Here's my reading.

In the Garden of Eden, the sexes enjoy parity. Eve is flesh of Adam's flesh, which indicates not dependency, but equality. She is what Adam couldn't find in all the other creatures. Then Eve, thanks to the serpent, puts Adam into the unfortunate predicament of having to choose between his girl and God. He decides to prize solidarity and union with her over his friendship with God. God appears, and punishment is meted out. Eve will suffer the pain of childbirth; Adam will live by the sweat of his brow; and the same will be true of their sons and daughters.

So far, so familiar. But then there's the puzzling line about how Eve "will lie in wait for the man." What does that mean?

My interpretation is that where once there was parity, now there is something uneven: the woman will look to the man for esteem and approval. That is the new, post-Fall reality.

Here's a classic example. A while back, we screened a film at the CIC about human trafficking in New York City. The filmmakers interviewed thirteen-, fourteen-year-old girls with the same sort of story: they were picked up by men who were in their twenties, seduced with meals and attention, used for sex, and then used eventually by the pimps' "friends." It happened over and over. Sometimes the girls would leave one trafficker for another, apparently not having learned the lesson that this was how they were being goaded into sex for hire.

The point is that you could see from the testimony onscreen that these girls weren't dim. Most seemed quite sharp—about everything else. But about this, they were duped. The reason was that they relied on these men for their own opinion of themselves.

So you believe that excessive deference to men, and excessive dependence on men, are part of the punishment handed to women for the Fall?

Fr. Arne: Yes. Feminism of the kind we've known for decades—the hard-driving feminism of a Margaret Sanger, a Gloria Steinem, etc.—is coming from exactly that attempt to restore the parity of Eden. But the trouble is, you can't do it by making a woman more like a man. That's the terrible irony of widespread abortion and contraception. On the surface, these seem to enable women to act more like irresponsible men. But on a deeper level, they only make it easier for men to manipulate women.

This is also why the Holy Father's Letter on the *Genius of Women*, mentioned earlier, is so vital. It says that women shouldn't mimic men or downplay their own nature and contribution in the world. But that's exactly what happens all the time.

I'm thinking of a man I saw just the other day, a devout father with four children. His wife is dedicated to her career—so much so that she's just gone to live in another city, coming home only on weekends. They live apart. I wonder what will come of it.

Same for commuter marriage?

Fr. Arne: I see commuter marriage as a kind of détente, less than as a real relationship. Is it a total disaster? No. It's better than getting divorced.

Let me offer what might be a friendly amendment to your obser-vations about the phenomenon of modern women mimicking men. Maybe this mimicry is, in effect, protective coloration. As of the sexual revolution, it's a predators' market out there. Maybe adopting male dress and male competition in the economic space, and male characteristics of swagger and brusqueness, are in part attempts to hide femininity—so as reduce the chances of being preyed upon. It needn't be conscious, and probably isn't. But it could be part of this picture.

Fr. Arne: Understanding the relationship between this trend and original sin is important to understanding reality. What we call feminism is the attempt to flee from both of the pun-ishments handed to Eve: the pain of procreation, and the pain of turning to men for approval and self-esteem. Because what we're talking about here is original sin, the project can't succeed.

18

Metaphysics and Modernity

Editor's note: On June 12, 2017, editor Rusty Reno of *First Things* organized a day-long colloquium in Washington, DC, to discuss a new paper by Fr. Thomas Joseph White, OP, on "The Metaphysics of Democracy."[1] Fr. Arne was otherwise engaged that day, and the subject of the conference was of particular interest to him, since it dealt in part with Newman's relationship to the liberal political order, as well as with larger questions of the relationship between the Church and democracy. We began the next morning with some thoughts about the conference.

There are many interesting threads we could follow from the colloquium yesterday. Here's one for starters. Fr. Thomas Joseph White argues that "modern secular democracy is failing," spiritually speaking, and that "the new trend toward nationalism will not be adequate to fill the void" because none of today's secular dogmas have staying power. He outlined the same shortcomings you've been identifying in these conversations—mainly, secularism's inability to fulfill the universal hunger for transcendence. He con-

---

[1] Fr. Thomas Joseph White, OP, "The Metaphysics of Democracy," *First Things*, February, 2018.

cludes that these continuing failures present a unique opportunity for the Church, and says that now is the time "to emphasize the deeper meaning of things, against the various sectarian dogmas of modern secular liberalism . . . by offering a rival version of modernity."

Your thoughts?

Fr. Arne: Fr. Thomas Joseph White dives in as a contemporary philosophical intellectual and quickly grasps what Brad Gregory says at the conclusion of the first long chapter in his book *The Unintended Reformation*, which is that modernity acts on a metaphysics of which it is entirely unaware—a deep subterranean force that's moving things beneath, so deep that it doesn't even stir the surface.[2] If it were to be made aware, modernity would deny that it has such an origin.

What's the essence of this modern metaphysics?

Fr. Arne: A complete relativism that makes man the center of all things, that makes man a God.

This was captured perfectly in the example of *Casey vs. Planned Parenthood* (1992), in the famous and infamous "mystery of life itself" phrase penned by Justice Anthony Kennedy: "At the heart of liberty is the right to define one's own concept of existence, of meaning, of the universe, and of the mystery of human life."

What's happened is that over the course of the last seven centuries, God has been pulled more into the world He created and transformed into the protagonist of this world. He is no longer entirely Other, as Aquinas would hold. Instead, via the

---

[2] Brad S. Gregory, *The Unintended Reformation: How a Religious Revolution Secularized Society*, 1st ed. (Princeton, NJ: Belknap Press, 2010).

loss of transcendence, he has become immanent. He's become us. We've become him. That's the aspiration of modernity. It's the ultimate original temptation.

There's a paradox there. These modern individuals are acting as gods and creators at the same time—yet they act as if there isn't a God. That intellectual tension is part of their problem.

Yesterday there was also discussion about whether liberalism has always been on a collision course with the Church—or whether something new has happened to put liberalism on a collision course with the Church. By "liberalism" is meant classical liberalism, of course.

Maybe liberalism has changed as of the sexual revolution, and has now become what we call progressivism. With apologies to Irving Kristol, one might say that a progressive is a liberal who's been mugged by the sexual revolution.

Fr. Arne: [laughs] It puts me in mind of that great quip by Malcolm Muggeridge back in 1966, that the Cross has been replaced by the orgasm as the epitome of human fulfillment. [Searches phone.] Here are some of his quotes about that; they're too good to overlook:

—"Sex is the ersatz or substitute religion of the twentieth century."

—"The orgasm has replaced the cross as the focus of longing and the image of fulfillment."

—"Sex is the mysticism of materialism and the only possible religion in a materialistic society."

—"The most terrible thing about materialism, even more terrible than its proneness to violence, is its boredom, from which sex, alcohol, drugs, all devices for putting out the accusing light of reason and suppressing the unrealizable aspirations of love, offer a prospect of deliverance."

And all of that, Muggeridge was seeing at what was actually just at the beginning of the sexual revolution.

One of the other shortcomings of progressivism, in addition to its grounding in the revolution, is its misguided belief in the positive direction of history. Think of the last question asked by Arthur Brooks of Robby George at the American Enterprise Institute gala in 2016. He said, "Robby, with all the darkness out there, how do you keep hope?" And Robby answered in part: "There is no right or wrong side of history; we're writing history here tonight."

The interaction of faith and grace in the lives of seven billion people is writing history right now. The progressive idea that this is all flowing toward progress affronts the Christian notion, taught by our Lord, that not all will be sweetness and light. The Bible describes the end times as something cataclysmic.

This brings us to another question about evil. When modern people talk about theodicy, or the problem of evil, they have in mind the example of the horse being beaten senselessly in Dostoevsky's Crime and Punishment; *or of cruelty to children; or other seemingly inexplicable suffering delivered to the innocent.*

But if we look at the twentieth century—the most violent the world ever saw—a different version of the problem of evil suggests itself: namely, what kind of deluded view of the world must one have in order to deny that evil exists?

How can anyone look at the record of the world wars and the Holocaust, the Gulag, the Cultural Revolution, and plenty else, and not grasp that the concept of evil is essential to explaining these things? The mere fact of the twentieth century would seem to be a stumbling block for atheism and agnosticism, on a scale that didn't exist before.

Fr. Arne: It's interesting. If you go back to our own beginnings, there were American founders who were very pro-French—of course Jefferson, but also to a lesser degree Madison. They talked about the French Revolution. The bloodshed, decapitations, guillotines, murder of the royalty, etc.: they regarded these as necessary evils. Hamilton was appalled by that view. But Jefferson and other Francophiles thought it was just part of the process of building a better society in France.

The only way to benignly condone all the horrors and evils is to interpret them as a path to a greater good—otherwise, they could never be countenanced. Think about what Thomas More writes in his *Utopia*, about heaven on earth that we can strive for.

Let's face it. Redemption took place through the Crucifixion of our Lord. There was something of itself that was objectively gruesome, painful, violent. The good of redemption came out of it, yes. However, you can see how it's possible to try and graft that notion, of good coming out of evil, onto other ideas about the future.

As for our constant self-delusion: as mentioned the devil remains the father of lies, the scatterer, the breaker of unity.

At yesterday's colloquium, two general lines of thought seemed to emerge. Some participants, including a Canadian theologian who focused on threats to religious liberty, believe that liberalism is now engaged in combat with religious practice.

Fr. Arne: It's amazing how acerbically anti-Catholic and anti-Christian the world has become.

At a time when so many people don't understand the Christian story, it would seem there's an especially pressing place for serious work: the arts. If we need witnesses more than teachers, that means arts colonies, stages, plays, movies, musicians—a parallel infrastructure to the secular monopoly on all that. Theologians and philosophers like to get back to metaphysics. With more attention focused on the arts, maybe Christianity's "rival vision" would become more vivid.

Fr. Arne: You know, it's interesting. We had a workshop for priests recently after Easter, and the speaker was Jonathan Reyes of the US Bishops' Conference. He was saying about evangelization that you can't give a natural law reason to people who are working on the level of mythological vision, and that we need to address this challenge.

It's what our Lord does. He tells parables. He tells stories. Raw reason doesn't work, often, because people are suspicious of it; and because it's a tool that more and more of them haven't been trained to use. The alternative is working on the mind, gut, heart—the empathetic whole. Think of how Tolkien is so effective. Finding that, developing that, is an important part of contemporary outreach.

The effectiveness of the Inklings, Tolkien and Lewis, et al., is all the more interesting because they were themselves working in a largely secular, sometimes hostile environment. Yet they were able to succeed in reaching beyond it, in part because they were working in community—regularly sharing work with one another, discussing ideas together.[3]

Fr. Arne: Back in the day when I was at Stanford, I organized a seminar. *Zen and the Art of Motorcycle Maintenance* had recently come out, and it had become a national sensation. *Time* and others treated it as the best thing since *Moby Dick*. It sounds like a passing phenomenon, but really, it's a recognizable story—one of a guy trying to find himself. It tracks Plato's *Phaedrus* and concerns similar questions: the importance of rhetoric, the meaning of love.

I put this together in the seminar with other works revolving around those questions. I had them watch *My Dinner with Andre*, another popular treatment of the meaning of life in which one character, playwright Wally, sees the world differently after his encounter with the other character, also a playwright. He realizes that he doesn't have to go around the world to find reality; it's right there in his life in the Bronx. We talked about all that, and then we read the *Phaedrus*, and Joseph Pieper's *Enthusiasm and Divine Madness*, a critique of the *Phaedrus*. Then we read C. S. Lewis's *The Four Loves*, and next, John Paul II's *Love and Responsibility*.

It was all good fun, but it was also a way of reaching people who might have been harder to reach in other ways and engaging them with the recognizable idea that everyone is driven toward love, real or counterfeit. As one participant said to me, "I agree with what you're saying—but it's diametrically opposed to everything that everyone else talks about on campus, in my courses, etc." He wasn't much, religiously speak-

---

[3] See Carol and Philip Zaleski, *The Fellowship: The Literary Lives of the Inklings: J.R.R. Tolkien, C.S. Lewis, Owen Barfield, Charles Williams* (New York: Farrar, Straus, and Giroux, 2015).

ing; he had little background in faith. But he was interested because the works all spoke to universal longing.

People are hungry and searching. A community for them doesn't have to be an established isolate. You can institute a place for them in your backyard. Some people regard the CIC as a spiritual oasis. I dispute that. It's a spiritual beachhead instead. It's a place where one can come to reload, relax, and go back out into the battle.

Having a critical mass is a powerful thing. You dip people into it, and they come out transformed, with a greater awareness of a life larger than what they've been living.

We can also make jujitsu of the record of modernism and postmodernism. Ugly architecture, ugly painting, ugly music, ugly everything: Just as telling a story to people can capture their attention, putting real art in front of them—figuratively, literally—can transform people from within.

Fr. Arne: This is something Fr. Barron develops well in his series on Catholicism.[4]

Everything is so blasted out there, on so many levels, that there are loose bricks all over the place, just waiting to be used to build something else. Maybe that's the case for hope.

Fr. Arne: There's no doubt that within all this detritus, the seeds of moving people elsewhere will be found. The aesthetic is something that people are always drawn to. They're drawn to what's actually beautiful and attractive.

---

[4] Robert Barron, *Catholicism*, available from https://www.youtube.com/watch?v=d_ScnCHiN1w.

Speaking of ruin, here's one other subject that came up at the col-
loquium about which it would be interesting to get your thoughts.
Many people have written off the possibility of Christian renewal
in Europe.

Fr. Arne: The question is whether there's sufficient critical
mass left to be harnessed. In France you have pockets of young
people, certainly in the South of France, especially, forming
small groups; Fr. Jacques Philippe and the Community of the
Beatitudes are another example. Even Paris has pockets of
practicing faith. The question is, will these efforts die on the
vine, because of depopulation?

In northern Europe, wolves are infiltrating back into places
where they've been banished for many centuries—because the
human footprint is diminishing. And then within Germany
. . . after listening to Mark Riebling discuss his book *Church
of Spies*, debunking the notion that Pius XII did not support
the Jews, I wonder whether what is going on in Germany may
not be the remnant of evil.[5] Pius XII we now know was in on
some of the assassination plots.

The attempts that failed against Hitler were amazing. He
did things he ordinarily wouldn't do that took him out of the
line of danger, several times, when he clearly would have been
dead under his usual routine. He was the instrument, I think,
or the pawn of something much larger than he was. There was
a positive power protecting him.

Does that evil genie continue to rule in Germany? In
terms of economic stability and prowess, it's one of the most
powerful countries; but at the same time, religious sentiment

---

[5] Mark Riebling, *Church of Spies: The Pope's Secret War against Hitler* (New
York: Basic Books, 2015).

is anti-Catholic, and even within the Catholic Church itself, prelates there have problems.

One final question suggested by the colloquium. In the rearview mirror, one sees clearly in the example of Germany which prelates stood up against Hitler and which didn't—who went to jail, who lost their lives or positions, etc. Do we need the bishops of America to take more of a stand on the issues of our own time, as several philosophers and theologians were arguing yesterday?

Fr. Arne: There's an exhibit on John Fisher at the John Paul II Center right now.[6] The saint's dying words were about being "the King's servant, but God's first." Those within the hierarchy do a lot—preach the Gospel, teach, administer the sacraments, sanctify the laity. But the real work of bringing the teachings of the Gospel into the public square—public sector, family life—is in the laity's hands.

So the Church is not just the prelates of the Church. And this, again, is one of the legacies of Vatican II that is still only just being assimilated. Many people thought that when the Church spoke of incorporating the laity, that meant as altar servers, lectors, in giving them ecclesiastical jobs, etc. John Paul II said: We've clericized the laity and laicized the clergy. But that's not how it should be.

Arthur Brooks gave a graduation talk at The Heights School[7] that made this point. He said to them: *Go where you're not invited, make what you're doing as natural as the*

---

[6] "God's Servant First: The Life and Legacy of Sir Thomas More," a collection of artifacts, was on display at the John Paul II Center between September 2016 and March 2017, available from https://www.catholicvirginian.org/?p=2928.

[7] The Heights School is a private, independent, preparatory school for boys in Potomac, Maryland. It provides a traditional liberal arts curriculum. Its

air you breathe. You need to be subversive Catholics. He gave examples. He spoke of a theoretical physicist he interviewed before a secular scientific audience. Arthur noticed that the physicist had a doctorate in theology and asked him to talk about that too—which had to be quite surprising to the rest of the audience; but the physicist spoke forthrightly about the importance of God in his life.

The other point is, don't try to rack up conquests. Don't try to implant the Cross on anyone, unless you're an exorcist. Arthur gave another example of a man who wrote to him, and called him a liar and a fraud, and otherwise took issue with his latest book. To which Arthur's response was positive: "Great, he read my book!" And he wrote the man to thank him for reading it, only to receive a return email saying: "If you're ever in Dallas, let's have lunch."

That's the point. That's the role of the laity. That's what happened in the early Church. Rodney Stark is another scholar who has studied how the Church grew under Roman persecution.[8] It's not just doctrine that keeps Christianity alive. There clearly was a sense in the early Church of closeness to Christ.

Think of the Apostles during those forty days of the risen Christ, experiencing his friendship, after the tragedy of his death, and wanting to share what they knew with the world. This is what fueled the early Church—friendship with Christ.

Christian orientation and spiritual formation are entrusted to Opus Dei, a personal prelature of the Catholic Church.

[8] Rodney Stark, *The Rise of Christianity: How the Obscure, Marginal Jesus Movement Became the Dominant Religious Force in the Western World in a Few Centuries* (San Francisco: HarperSanFrancisco, 1997).

19

Some Questions about God and Caesar

Let's talk a little about politics. You've given spiritual direction to nationally known politicians. Many people now think the United States has reached a critical moment in which ideological division has become so much worse than expected until very recently. Yesterday's shooting of a congressman at a baseball game is just the latest terrible example.[1]

Fr. Arne: The question is: Under what circumstances is it impermissible for a Catholic to vote for a candidate?

There is, for starters, the lesser-of-two-evils camp. Take this last election. No one really liked either of the candidates. Hillary's supporters would be quick to point out that she won the popular vote. But they really overlooked everyone in flyover country. This whole business of the oligarchy

---

[1] On June 14, 2017, Congressman Steve Scalise of Louisiana (R) was shot and gravely wounded by left-wing activist James Thomas Hodgkinson while practicing for the annual Congressional Baseball Game for Charity. Three others present were shot as well. Hodgkinson died of wounds after being shot by police. Those attacked have recovered.

assuming that they know best, that we live in a nanny state, and that the upper twenty percent should be telling everyone else who's uneducated and unwashed how to live, what they should do, how they should think, how they need to be taken care of. . . . Certainly, a lot of people resented that and recognized that this attitude had been part of the status quo for a long time. It really goes back to, say, the election of John F. Kennedy, and the sense of an elite intelligentsia that runs the country and understands what's best for it.

Where do you think that idea came from in the first place? Is it partly a function of television?

Fr. Arne: Certainly, the media has played a large part in it. I think also Charles Murray's *Coming Apart* makes the point that back in the day, the executive of a company could have breakfast at the local grill with the guy who's a foreman there; and they could be sitting and chatting at the same table.[2] There was much more of a sense of integration. Now that could never happen.

Back in those days, you had a polity, and even television news was news, not *People* magazine. There was a much larger sense that the news was communicating information worldwide, and with some kind of organized intellectual content, not just spectacle. Today's news doesn't give you something to talk about with others. So I suppose the divide began when you really needed a college education to be able to carry on a discussion. Common conversation became trivialized. There came a self-perpetuating dynamic whereas the decades wore on, the oligarchy became more entrenched.

---

[2] Charles Murray, *Coming Apart: The State of White America, 1960–2010* (New York: Crown Forum, 2012).

I thought that the article I gave you recently from *Harvard* magazine, about the class divide that's become so vivid since our last election, was interesting.[3] Everyone wants to talk about racism. No one wants to address the elephant in the room, which is the class divide, and the elite's dismissiveness of the rest of the country.

It seems these days that people want a candidate who listens to them. But of course properly understood a candidate shouldn't be just a sounding board; politicians are leaders who make decisions. For a Catholic or any other voter who just wants their vote to do some good, what becomes impermissible to vote for?

Fr. Arne: For a Catholic, someone who holds as public policy something that is inimical to the public good as understood and presented by the social teaching of the Church. Some would argue that one has to balance these things. What if both candidates strongly support abortion? Writing in a ballot may be a nice gesture, but it's completely ineffectual. So for whom do you vote?

The question itself points to a deeper problem. When you reach the point where you don't have a candidate and the question is, which is the better of the two rather than which one do I not vote for. . . . There are great guys in the pipeline for 2020, 2024, who look a lot better than the candidates we just had.

So politics isn't an entire wasteland. Getting people while they're ascending and still teachable is important to transforming the culture. That's part of why I'm hopeful.

Back to the question: there's no easy answer. If someone thought we should export all the Jews in the United States,

---

[3]   Richard D. Kahlenberg, "Harvard's Class Gap: Can the Academy Understand Donald Trump's Forgotten Americans?," *Harvard*, May–June 2017.

that, obviously, would be a candidate impermissible for a Catholic to support. Ratchet that down. The pro-life issue is major, because the well-being of a society is its attention to the future. If you're only trying to solve yesterday's problems, you're in a bad way. There has to be a sense of building for the next generation and doing so with a sense of hope. What's the hope of the future? Children.

So obviously, if a platform is open to eliminating future citizens, including without any care for their potential contributions, that's inimical to society's flourishing. I've pointed out to Peter Thiel that he targets the demise of technological growth in this country around 1973. *Roe vs. Wade* was 1973. Think about it: How many—sixty, seventy million children who have never seen the light of day? Might there not have been some changes on account of that? Couldn't one of those unborn citizens have gotten a handle on the cure for cancer?

The economic tax base, we now know, has become very dangerous, an inverted pyramid. Eliminating all those people has also had a significant economic impact.

The point is that the pro-life issue isn't just a religious issue, as many nonreligious people like to make it. It has to do with policy, with the future of the country, with the common good. And it's important to explain these deep ramifications, because it's become so easy for people to dismiss the pro-life position as "just" a religious issue. No: it has to do with the well-being and success of this country. And people who don't see that need to go back to re-education camp.

Many Catholics remain confused about whether it is ever permissible to vote for a candidate who's pro-abortion. Any guidance for them?

Fr. Arne: It helps to ask what level of politician we're talking about. Is this about a vote for President? For Congress? For the local school board? If it's the local school board, a person's stand on that question isn't going to be significant. It's different when you're talking about holding the highest office in the land. The point is that you have to see how their views will impact what they're capable of doing in the office they seek. Obviously the higher the office, the more critical will be their stand.

Thus far, we've been talking about voters, and their considerations about how to vote. What about the question of politicians who are pro-abortion, public Catholics?

Fr. Arne: It's interesting. When the question comes up about the Church doing more about this, we're back to the matter of the laity, and the laity being the Church too. The teaching of the Gospel in the public square is the role of the lay faithful. They can go where priests and bishops can't. It's about being a good professional—a good example—that gives you credibility with people in the public square. Think of a good mother, who balances professional life and family life in a positive way, and what kind of example she becomes to others. The message of the Second Vatican Council, as we've been discussing, is that the lay faithful need to be helped to be good witnesses.

A few years ago, Archbishop Chaput was in town, speaking about his book *Render unto Caesar*,[4] and afterwards at dinner one of the guests made the point to him that the Church needs to do more to correct prominent Catholics who

---

[4] Charles J. Chaput, *Render unto Caesar: Serving the Nation by Living Our Catholic Beliefs in Political Life* (New York: Doubleday Religion, 2008).

give scandal by misrepresenting and violating Church teaching. And Archbishop Chaput responded, "This is the role of
the lay faithful."

People inside and outside the Church need to understand
that the Church is not just the hierarchy. The faith is transformative, and the laity has a unique role witnessing to that reality.

Any other reflections on politics?

Fr. Arne: From early times on, politics comes up. Render unto
Caesar was the beacon for all times when it comes to understanding how to deal with the questions of politics. One can
say there are things that are in the interests both of Caesar and
of God; and the Church has always recognized as much. The
family, education, questions of life and death, health care: all
are areas in which there's shared interest, and they're some of
the more difficult things to work out to get to who should have
the last say. The Church says ultimately that she, the Church,
should; but the whole question of marriages and marriage
licenses in the same-sex marriage issue raised the question of
whether there should even be a civil and religious act separately.

What do you think?

Fr. Arne: I think it can be argued both ways. But if the Church
has to be forced to perform same-sex weddings. . . . In Arlington, Virginia I had to get a certificate before signing a marriage
license, to get certified as a minister. Could I be forced to have
to perform marriage to anyone who asked? Some would argue
the Church should get out of the marriage business by not
having priests and deacons be officials of the state. I can see
that being a possibility.

Consider the whole business of caesaropapism. After the peace of Constantine and the edict of Milan in AD 313, the Church went from being persecuted to privileged overnight. If you were a Christian in those early centuries, you put your life on the line, your money on the line; persecutions and purges were real. Then overnight it changed, and everyone wanted in. That was a beginning of the loosening of *praxis*, the "Catholic-in-name-only," and that's when the monastic orders began to have people living apart from the world.

And this is true down through the ages. In the tenth century, the practice of papal investiture, when political leaders would choose who would be bishop and so on, gave an unhealthy amount of the Church to the authorities. China is the same in our day. When the papal states were lost in 1870, many thought it was catastrophe; but others were applauding. Some über-Catholics thought this was the end of the world, but more reasonable ones thought it was a breath of fresh air.

This separation of Church and Caesar brings up a question particularly pertinent these days. A handful of Christian colleges take no federal money so that they're free to teach what they teach without interference from the state: Hillsdale College, Grove City, Wyoming Catholic, and a couple of others. Do you think that's the wave of the future? Do you think more and more institutions of higher education will have to choose between their Christianity and their desire for federal support?

Fr. Arne: I do; and it's true not only for colleges, but also for hospitals.

There's an irony in all this. The Church has historically taken a leading role in both education and health care. Universities were begun by the Church. Hospitals were begun by the Church. Progressives want to tar the Church with being anti-intellectual, anti-science. It's a shibboleth. George Weigel has just published a piece pointing out that Gregor Mendel and Georges Lemaitre, the founders of modern genetics, were not only Catholics, but priests.[5] Is the Church against "gender" issues? Well, the Church was the first to understand gender [laughs].

So that the Church would be put in the position of not taking funding for these things which the Church started in the first place. . . . Well, it's like the marriage issue: If it comes to that, it comes to that. But I think it's vital to recognize the contributions that the Church has made in these fields, and to be cognizant that if you start pulling the Church out of them, your health care becomes much more precarious, especially with end-of-life issues and abortion; and education loses its metaphysical underpinnings because of the incredible miasma of relativism we're dealing with today.

I'm not saying all education has to be faith-based. But there are great truths that are at risk of being lost.

Josef Pieper, one of my favorite philosophers, makes the point that philosophers begin with what's around them, saying that they leave no stone unturned in finding the truth; and that the Greek philosophers, for example, asked very basic questions about reality. They didn't have revelation. Why, today, rule out revelation as a potential source of truth? A philosopher should leave no stone unturned.

This brings up another question related to politics and the role of Church vs. state: the so-called end-of-life issues. I was in London

---

[5] George Weigel, "Way Beyond the New Atheist Nonsense," *First Things*, June 14, 2017.

*a few years ago, and there was a referendum of some sort about
euthanasia. Everywhere one looked, billboards and buses and
other sources sported ads urging the killing of the old and sick.
Fr. Arne, you're sick. Does that reality change your way
of looking at these matters? Does it sharpen matters, one way
or another? Euthanasia is so front and center these days. Any
insights?*

Fr. Arne: Yes.

What's pointed out always is that killing must be permitted because "we don't want them to suffer." And that's a crock.
Modern medicine is capable of pain management very, very
well. I know; I'm a prime example of that experience right now.

So let's be real about what's behind calls for euthanasia.
The issues are, one: cost. Will this spend the person's entire
estate? Will there be anything left for the children? Two: hassle.
If Mom or Grandmom is alive, there's a certain expectation
that the children will be around somewhere; but if there have
been estrangements or if it's been painful to deal with Mom, or
both, and she's not going to get better, there's an expectation
of "let's just end this." The state obviously has a vested interest
also; the greatest amount of money poured into a patient is
typically in the last year and a half of life.

So I'd say it's not so much about the patient as about the
environment—Medicare, insurance, and the family, with all
these different sources asking, "What's it going to cost us?"

And of course these anxieties and worries are mapped
onto the patient. The patient is told that their care is expensive,
and can't help but think, *Little John or Jean could have all their
college education paid for, instead of it going down the drain into
my medical expenses.*

And of course what's most of all a factor in these calcula-
tions is loneliness. With the small families that have become
typical, people are more isolated. They may have brought it on
themselves by their choices, or they may not have. Either way,
it's difficult to be alone. Nursing homes are usually pitiable,
places where people are doped and lollygagging in front of the
television, wheeled around like objects, etc.

So in my case, I'm at death's door [laughs], and I'm having
some of the best moments of my life. What can I say? [laughs].
Obviously, one's attitude has a lot to do with faith. It's not faith,
family, and finances that matter; it's family and faith. That's
what makes all the difference in the world.

That's an arresting way of framing the issue. We're typically told
that euthanasia has become thinkable because humanity has now
learned to prolong life so far that serious problems are bound to
emerge. What you're saying is, no: that euthanasia is a conse-
quence of the fracturing of the family; that this fracturing has as
much to do with its momentum as any scientific advance.

Fr. Arne: Yes. Similarly, the so-called overpopulation issue,
which gets rolled out every decade or so, isn't science. The
wealth of nation lies in its citizens. Again, out of the many
who have never seen daylight since 1973: say it's a million
a year. In the course of all that, there must have been many
extraordinary individuals who could have made a contribution
to society—if they'd had a chance.

That's what is so strange about seeing euthanasia pushed so much
in Western countries, especially. We've already got abortion. We've
got contraception. We have an aging population. Now we want

euthanasia. What more can you give people who seem to want to disappear?

Fr. Arne: Here's a little thought experiment. I often point out that in the human ecology, abortion, and marriage examples, you have to give the devil credit.

Let's take ecology. If humanity is a cancer on the face of the earth, take it off. If you have cancer, you don't go to your doctor and say, take half of it off. No: you want it all off.

What's the goal of people seeking contraception and abortion? They may not consciously will it, but we know now that these trends as seen today may bring humanity's fecundity down to such a level that ultimately, you're getting rid of everybody. Not today or tomorrow of course; but in the final analysis, when rates fall below replacement and stay there, it will amount to erasing humanity. Look at Japan.

And then there's same-sex marriage. It's not about engendering the future, either.

All of these become examples of ending the human story. So who, exactly, has an interest in ending that story? God knows that some of his creatures aren't going to get to heaven. But that doesn't keep him from bringing life into the world. The devil, on the other hand, gets ticked off every time even one of the creatures gets to heaven. His best strategy is to end the game. It's just a thought experiment! But there's a logic there.

20

Catholic Doctrine for (Non) Dummies

Fr. Arne, today let's imagine that you're speaking directly to a secular audience. Let's try to do a reverse Dan Brown, and de-scarify or demystify a few items that you've been explaining to people throughout your priesthood. Our readers without religious background might find it interesting to see a mini-primer here. Many Protestants as well as secular people have issues with the idea of the communion of saints, for example—or saints, period. Maybe you could clarify some of that teaching for people unfamiliar with it.

Fr. Arne: I was going through our notes and seeing how the point about a body of fellow travelers comes up over and over; how the idea of the individual becomes the apogee of human perfection; and how we've lost the sense of relation-ality because of it. This is one of the great problems of our time.

Recall our talk earlier about the Beatles in Central Park, people united by interested in their music. By contrast, imagine St. Peter's Square. You have a panoply of languages from around the world; but there's a greater sense of community than in an all-English setting like the Beatles concert. How do you explain that? It's not merely a sociological phenomenon. The Holy Spirit has something to do with it.

The Church is composed of three elements: the Church triumphant, meaning those who have made it to heaven and crossed that finish line; the Church militant, meaning those of us who are still struggling; and then the Church being purified by those who are in between, in Purgatory, getting cleaned up, as it were, to enter the community of saints in heaven.

Again, the whole Enlightenment project exalted something else: the individual, making the individual the unit they're dealing with. So understanding some of these things we've been talking about, intercessory prayer, for example, becomes harder—because of that rigid focus on the individual. Outside the garage there [pointing out the window], for example, is a section of sidewalk in miserable disrepair. Some of the guys here sent requests to different people in the city administration, mayor's office, city council, etc., without much response. Now, if you happen to know personally the nephew of the mayor, or someone who's connected, your chances of getting that attended to are much greater.

In some ways the communion of saints is dealing with those people who have clearly manifested their friendship with Christ, and thereby provide more open access to having requests fulfilled more expeditiously than any old wayward stranger or sinner who's just straggling along.

That's the utilitarian approach to explaining the communion of saints. But the deeper point is the bond. One of the priests I know who's in Rome working on his doctorate is studying priestly fraternity, the idea that we priests are truly brothers in Christ. We are sons of the same Father, for one thing. A lot of people talk about the friendship among priests, and how important it is, and it's true.

But fraternity is a deeper union than friendship. Brothers may fight with one another, but they'd never fight among themselves outside; and if anyone from outside attacks one brother, they'll have the other brothers coming after them. Fraternity is a bond that is beyond voluntary association. That, too, is part of the community of saints.

How about the sacraments? Secular people—and others—have trouble understanding what Catholics mean by sacraments, as opposed to mere ritual. Anything you'd like to throw out about that?

Fr. Arne: Sacraments are the vestiges of Christ present in our time. They are fingerprints or footprints of Christ's continuing presence in our time. It's not that he's some figure from the past who's come and gone. He is still present, in the sacraments.

It's most palpable in the Eucharist, and also in Confession. It is Christ who baptizes, Christ who witnesses a marriage. So the external sign, in the case of the Eucharist, is bread and wine; in Baptism, water; in Confirmation, oil; in marriage, a contract being witnessed by God. In all of these things, there's an external physical sign that mimics the internal effect of that.

What about explaining the Eucharist?

Fr. Arne: Now, people ask me: Do you really believe all that? Do you really think that is the body and blood of Christ?

We're dealing with a mystery here, since there's obviously nothing parallel in nature. And to understand it, you need metaphysical understanding. The terms "substance" and "accident" are foreign to the modern, materialistic, mechanistic mind.

But think of understanding by way of analogy: when the priest says the words of consecration, there is nothing visibly, physically different about what is before him than what had been there two minutes ago. What the Church does believe is that the substance has changed; and that the appearance, or what classical Aristotelian logic would call "accidental" characteristics, is exactly as it was before. The Church holds that the reality underlying that has radically changed. Those accidental characteristics localize where our Lord is. The accidents are somehow miraculously sustained no longer by the substance of bread and wine but by a miracle of God.

Now clearly, the Jewish people who heard our Lord speak in John 6 were scandalized. Christ uses a word for eating that makes clear he is not talking about some figurative act, but the literal act of eating.

There are Eucharistic miracles, collected in books, about what has happened to Hosts. In one case in Argentina that has been tested by science, a Host left in a glass transformed into the DNA of a Middle Eastern man in his thirties. In another case, a priest who didn't believe in the Real Presence put a piece of bread in the chalice, and it began to bleed. This was in Italy.

There are books about these miracles which narrate these phenomena in which God has taken an extra step to give a physical, tangible manifestation of what believers hold.

When secular people hear that kind of story, they tend to write it off as so much nonsense. It's interesting to turn the tables here and there, and to look at what secularism itself puts faith in. Consider the rise of the ghost story in England, a genre whose growth exactly parallels the decline of Christian practice. Many modern people might think Christianity is bunkum—but there they are, believing instead that a banshee is wailing on top of Grandma's country house.

Ghost stories are similar to spiritualism, another body of beliefs not exactly rooted in empiricism that took off just as Christianity seemed to be diminishing, and that was led by a particularly tony crowd, at that—Arthur Conan Doyle, William James. Joseph Bottum has deployed the nice phrase, "bastard Christianities"[1]*; and of course, in some sense all these variants are bastard offsprings of Christianity. So one thing you might do here is give people a bridge to Catholic thinking—because people do believe in ghosts, they do believe in angels and demons—and it might be interesting for them to learn how Christianity has explained such things.*

Fr. Arne: Globally, they reflect the fact that despite our materialism and mechanistic thinking, there's still a sense that reality is about more than the measurable—that we're not just machines. There's clearly more to the world than meets the naked eye or the five senses. And as much as we try to contain everything in that mechanistic model, something always ends up squeaking out because the model isn't commensurate with the world itself. It's like the leaky dike. Something always gets out to remind us that our paradigm doesn't fit.

What about people who believe they've seen a ghost, or had some other perceived spectral experience? What does the Church say? Is she agnostic about that?

Fr. Arne: No. The Church has always recognized the possibility of spirits returning. When St. Peter is released from prison, chained and under guard, and he ends up back in the house

---

[1] Joseph Bottum, *An Anxious Age: The Post-Protestant Ethic and the Spirit of America* (New York: Image, 2014), 108.

where they're all praying for him, their first impulse is that it must be Peter's angel. People of his time, and earlier, clearly had a sense of an angelic world.

The Church has always recognized that there are created spirits that are pure being, with an intuitive intellect much more powerful than ours. That's why their decisions for or against God are absolute, as opposed to ours which are kind of muddling. The decision to rebel against God is taken by them with clear understanding of the consequences. Now, it's said that angels were not given beatific vision—that they were not able to see God as they would in eternity, or they'd have been unable to choose against him. Of course, this is all speculation, but there's a logic in it. Because we human beings reason in a slow plodding fashion, we can go back and change our minds; whereas the angels don't have that weakness, and can't go back.

Old Testament Jews and New Testament Christians have always had a sense of a world of spirits, some of which we guess at, and some of which is experiential. What's a ghost coming back? Well, it could be the sense of souls in Purgatory, coming back to ask for prayers. Ghost tales usually are premised on the idea that the protagonists have unfinished business, that they're trying to communicate something to someone on earth. Purgatory could fit with that.

The flip side of that kind of supernatural experience is that of visitation—being visited by someone dead, in a reassuring way. Anthropologists have made the point that visitation dreams are part of the reason people believe in God in the first place—because these experiences are apparently near-universal. Does the Church say anything in particular about that?

Fr. Arne: To my knowledge, no. The Church has always been very cautious about para-phenomena, because it's so hard to test them—they're usually unique. Or think of Marian apparitions. Lourdes, Fatima, and a few others are accepted formally, but not many. The Church doesn't necessarily reject the others. But she is very careful about giving her bona fides in cases that aren't seen by more than one person, or that won't have a positive effect, or other criteria. There is private revelation— the Lord, the saints, Our Lady can appear to many. But the Church is careful not to create a world of para-phenomena for people to glom onto.

People are always looking for the unusual, the strange in religion. Whereas, in fact, the heroism of everyday repetition is much more powerful, even though it doesn't have the glamor of apparitions and the rest. Let's face it. On the Fourth of July, you may enjoy the Marine band playing—but everyone's really there for the fireworks.

Popular interest in all those exorcist and possession movies would seem to be additional evidence that contemporary men and women aren't always as far from the religious reservation as they think. People just can't let it go. They do believe in these things, even though they may not admit it to themselves.

Fr. Arne: It's interesting to consider what happens with possession. There are, for whatever reason, a number of exorcism cases in southern Maryland, for example. They seem to be predominately cases involving young women. It's not that a person who is possessed is a heinous sinner. Sometimes the individual is trying to lead a holy life—but they really are under attack, under siege, with manifestations that are clearly para-phenomenal, like strength beyond one's physical capacity.

Our Lord deals with this, obviously. I also know of examples from the Caribbean, voodoo cases, where people gash themselves in what is clearly a form of possession.

These phenomena, for whatever reason, tend to be more common among the worst-off. We shouldn't be afraid to name the devil, because it's much easier for evil to do its work when people refuse to identify it.

People do come to me with questions about dreams and such; but possession, no. Even priests who are involved with exorcism are careful—every diocese has an exorcist, but it's a very restricted group. Everyone recognizes that this is dangerous stuff. Not only is the person possessed under attack, but also those who perform exorcisms; their faith, chastity, and so on will come under attack. The devil wants to pull all of them away from God.

Many people also struggle to understand what the Church teaches about miracles, including the sort that are used to argue for beatification and canonization—i.e., miracles performed after an individual's death. How would you explain miracles to curious readers who may not have encountered these teachings?

Fr. Arne: It's interesting. There was a debate between Christopher Hitchens and Dinesh D'Souza during the heyday of the new atheism. D'Souza was speaking about the Resurrection, and Hitchens said, "There you go! Talking about miracles." D'Souza then turned the gun back on him, and said, "You're a scientist, aren't you? Can you name one law of science that knows of absolutely no exception?" There was a pause . . . and another pause. . . . Obviously, D'Souza's credibility was rising with each passing moment. Finally, Hitchens said no. D'Souza replied that miracles are among those exceptions that can't be explained.

About the intercession of saints: it's a tangible means by which God underwrites that this person is truly a friend of God, capable of drawing down God's favor. Think again of the example of getting the sidewalk fixed. Someone close to God has a better chance of interceding than any random individual.

It's tricky. Usually the miracles have to be medical miracles, physical miracles. Of course, spiritual conversion, getting someone back into the Church after thirty years away from the sacraments and the Church, say, might count as a miracle. But you can't really prove causality there. For example, in the case of the beatification of Portillo,[2] there was a woman in Chicago with a prayer card that he'd actually touched. She had lung cancer, and her lungs were full of metastases. The doctor had given her mere days. She had the prayer card and was calling out, "Álvaro! Álvaro!" The next day she went to the doctor for a scan, and there was nothing in her lungs.

Usually, a cure has to be spontaneous and permanent. Somewhere in Chile, meanwhile, a lad fell into a pool and was dead for thirty minutes. His family was praying to Álvaro for that time, and he came back. Coming back from the dead in a seemingly hopeless situation is powerful evidence for a miracle, and that one was used as evidence for the beatification of Álvaro.

Also considered as evidence is how many people are praying for a person's intercession at the same time.

---

[2] As mentioned earlier in chapter six, Blessed Álvaro del Portillo (1914–1994) was a Roman Catholic bishop who succeeded St. Josemaría Escrivà as the prelate of Opus Dei, serving between 1982 and 1994. He was beatified in 2014.

So, there's the emphasis on community again, including after death.

Fr. Arne: Yes. And of course it's complicated, because everyone can be praying to someone, so there has to be a general sense of recourse to a particular saint; and there's usually a physical aspect, like having been touched by something of the person's, for example, a relic. The Church is very careful with this evidence too.

21

Serenity and Grace in the Face of Death

Fr. Arne, it's the opinion of all your friends that few have handled the burdens of terminal illness more gracefully or serenely. Sooner or later, no matter what we believe, your readers and the rest of us will all be where you are now. What thoughts might you be interested in sharing about how to cope with sickness and the knowledge of imminent demise?

Fr. Arne: First, as said before: people with chronic disease, especially, must understand that their condition is a treasure to be administered for the benefit of others.

I have many doctor friends by now, and I tell them: with all due respect, in the long run, you're failures! [laughs]. At least in my line of work, we have a better rate of success—some of our patients get to live forever.

But as for living forever here on earth . . . If you read *Gulliver's Travels*, you find that every time there's a funeral procession in the Land of the Immortals, those watching it are wistful, and for good reason.

Now obviously, I'm not counseling euthanasia [laughs]. The point is that the body breaks down, and that breakdown tells us something. To want to live forever as a twenty-year-old isn't the same as thinking of carrying an old body into eternity.

I tell people who are ill that they need to be aware we're only passing through in this life. We're going somewhere else. The greatest part of our life is actually on the other side, as the Psalms repeatedly remind us.

Think of this image. Some people imagine that we walk down the corridor of life and then face two doors. That's true. But the doors aren't right next to each other. They're on opposite ends of the corridor. As you near the one door, there's a sense of peace, the idea that it's attractive to be drawing closer toward God. We see this peace in the lives of holy people on earth.

When you draw toward the other door, at the opposite end, you see something very different: people feeling miasma, anger, lethargy, melancholy, conflict.

So I think that what God does is give us a foretaste of heaven or hell while we're still on earth. Imagine you're at a gathering, like the kind we see so often in Washington. Someone of influence comes into the room, and people are slowly drawn toward him. Someone else of more influence comes in, and the crowd shifts in that direction instead.

We're drawn toward what's powerful, and we see it better and better as we near it—including toward the end of life. Hell is the pinnacle of narcissism. That's why people recoil, resist, and fight as they near it. Hell is isolation.

Sartre seems to have called that one exactly wrong.[1]

---

[1] Jean-Paul Sartre's 1944 play *No Exit* is best known for the line, "Hell is other people."

Fr. Arne: He did. And that reminds me: I have a friend who keeps a list in his pocket at all times of ten people who are worse off than he is. That's a great antidote to a pity party.

Fr. Arne, in transcribing and looking over our conversations, it's striking how polished your extemporaneous paragraphs appear in print. Did writing ever beckon you as a vocation?

Fr. Arne: I was too lazy! [laughs] Also, I felt it incumbent not to self-promote, or give the appearance of same. Of course many priests have blogs and books, etc.—sometimes excellent ones. And of course living in downtown Washington, with the closest tabernacle to the White House right there at the CIC, I'm not exactly trying to hide in the corner.

But St. Josemaría said, "When you get a letter, you throw away the envelope."

I feel the same. I'm the envelope.

Editor's note: Fr. Arne Panula died on July 19, 2017. His funeral Mass filled the Cathedral of St. Matthew the Apostle in downtown Washington, DC.

Recollections

I wanted to share the most profound thing Father ever said to me—and that is a high bar. . . . I was telling him in spiritual direction that I don't know what I'm going to say for myself when I die, and I have to face the Lord. And he said, softly and gently, "Father." It sent a shiver down my spine.

The other thing is perhaps my favorite memory of him. A couple of years ago he came to the parish fall festival at St. John the Beloved in McLean, Virginia. I was a volunteer, running around doing this and that. I took Fr. Arne into the kitchen to get him some water, and there was a girl from the parish there, probably eight or nine. She asked if I would help her carve a little pumpkin she was holding. I told her I would love to, but I had to get back to work.

Fr. Arne said, "I'll help you." He found a knife in the kitchen and started carving. As I was leaving, I could hear him say, "Isn't it amazing how God puts all these seeds into this little pumpkin?"

Friend and confidante to billionaires and Supreme Court Justices, carver of pumpkins.

—*A young professional living in Washington, DC*

*   *   *

Fr. Arne was my Director for nine years, starting in fall of 2008 when I moved to Washington to join the American Enterprise Institute. He immediately identified a key objective for me as the leader of a secular institution: to sanctify my work and help others to sanctify theirs as well. He asked me to meditate on this passage from "Passionately Loving the World," a homily delivered by St. Josemaría on October 8, 1967, at the University of Navarre:

> God is calling you to serve Him in and from the ordinary, material, and secular activities of human life. He waits for us every day, in the laboratory, in the operating theatre, in the army barracks, in the university chair, in the factory, in the workshop, in the fields, in the home, and in all the immense panorama of work. Understand this well: there is something holy, something divine, hidden in the most ordinary situations, and it is up to each one of you to discover it.

This collaborative message between Fr. Arne and St. Josemaría was the most powerful direction I have ever received, and indeed spawned the concept of "earned success" as the source of happiness that occupied much of my secular apostolate while at AEI.

The sanctification of my work was Fr. Arne's last lesson to me as my Director—two weeks after he died. Early in August of 2017, I received a call from Fr. Paul Scalia, who was organizing a retreat for priests eight months hence. This was a job previously undertaken by Fr. Arne, who helpfully left instructions for Fr. Paul to follow after his death. One of these instructions was to tell me that I would be serving as the lay speaker at that retreat, on the subject of the work of evangelization in everyday life. He had not told me, and his message was clear in this small act: that he would be watching over my work, and trusted I would sanctify it by dedicating it to the glory of our Lord.

—*Arthur Brooks, President, American Enterprise Institute*

*   *   *

I met Fr. Arne when I was a teenager. At the time, I was experiencing invasive thoughts, haunting visions, and the sensation of a dark presence following me. As a student at an Ivy League school, I did not feel that my peers would understand or even try to understand this kind of spiritual warfare. I felt particularly alone. Furthermore, I did not believe nor want to believe in a preternatural "evil," yet my daily life was plagued by inexplicable episodes, which made this time period all the more alienating and confusing. Needless to say, this was a frightening period for both my parents and me.

After one particularly harrowing sleepless night, I felt hopeless in the face of this nightmare. My mother brought me to the CIC for counsel. As soon as I met Fr. Arne, I immediately felt safe. As others have described, Fr. Arne's penetrating gaze was both unnerving in its intensity and reassuring, one of the most pure and deep expressions of love I have ever felt. To be in his presence was a full spiritual experience. . . . I felt that he could immediately see everything that was going on and could at once banish this presence and simultaneously channel God's unconditional love for me, the human vessel carrying these experiences. As we conversed and he was able to put words to my troubles, I felt a deep trust that everything was going to be okay. Unlike others, he was not frightened by what I had to tell him; he truly understood, and I got the sense that he had experience with, and mastery of, the kind of spiritual warfare being waged on the territory of my soul.

Whatever it was must have been frightened of Fr. Arne, too, because it did not bother me again. In every conversation we had henceforth, from those teenage years to his final days, his gaze brought tears to my eyes. It was as if he was fully in the presence of God with every word he spoke. I have never seen a more transparent human incarnation of God's love than in Fr. Arne.

—An artist from the DC area

*   *   *

I first met Fr. Arne shortly after converting to Catholicism when I found myself wandering through the bookstore at the Catholic Information Center (CIC). As a new convert, stumbling into the CIC by accident was like happening upon a theme park. As I perused the shelves, Fr. Arne approached me and kindly introduced himself. When he found out I was in town from New York, he told me he used to serve a priest there. He asked me about where I attended Mass in New York, congratulated me on my conversion, and wished me well.

A few years later I began to frequent DC on a more regular basis—often multiple times a month—and the CIC effectively became my home base. I'd stow luggage there, have impromptu meetings, and sometimes just hang out. It was during this time that I got to know Fr. Arne—never through formal spiritual direction, but simple friendship. He'd ask about my life, things I had recently written, and occasionally tease me that I should pay some portion of the CIC's rent. It was long after I had come to know Fr. Arne as the head of the CIC that I realized that he was a Harvard graduate, the one-time head of Opus Dei in the United States who led the organization's 47-million-dollar campaign to build new headquarters in New York, and a confessor to politicians and power brokers in our nation's capital.

For Fr. Arne, these details were insignificant. He embodied Pope Francis's description of priests who have the smell of their sheep. Some of his sheep smelt of Brooks Brothers attire and others just smelt more like Amtrak. And yet Fr. Arne didn't make a distinction, and cared for us all the same.

—*Christopher White, National Correspondent for the Catholic news site* Crux

*   *   *

The first time I met Fr. Arne I felt a little like Nathanael meeting Jesus. He already knew me. This was not just because—I found out later—he had been praying for me for several years after having been asked by others to do so, but also because he had an extraordinary capacity to see what was within others, to meet and understand them with affection, and to draw out the good. Meeting him was like finding a compass.

Our first conversation lasted no more than fifteen minutes, but left me transformed by his capacity to clarify, inspire, and direct, which I believe was a fruit of his cooperation with the gifts of the Holy Spirit. I feel very blessed that that conversation had many chapters, stretched out over years. He was like a master mechanic who, in only a few minutes, could not only give a thorough tune-up but upgrade you spiritually from a used jalopy to a new Mercedes. I learned so much from him about God, about myself, about the sanctification of daily life, about the priesthood, about spiritual direction and confession, and so much more.

—*Fr. Roger Landry, priest, New York*

*   *   *

I was just returning from Amherst, Massachusetts, where I was at work clearing out the house that our family had occupied for forty-five years, and I was counting on seeing Fr. Arne as soon as I'd returned. Fr. Arne Panula had been thought months earlier to have entered the last stages of the slow-moving cancer he had borne for about fifteen years.

The cancer had been slow moving, but Fr. Arne had not been. He had expanded dramatically the programs and reach of the Catholic Information Center on K Street; he had managed to reach so many young Catholic professionals and bring them into an expanded network of Catholic teaching and engagement. But he was now receding from the directorship of the Center, and we were told that he was now essentially moving into the conditions of hospice in the house he shared with other members of Opus Dei.

. . . I went to see him, expecting to find him in bed. Instead, he was on his feet, looking as engaged as ever, and ready as ever for a round of serious conversation. . . . He would later remark that these last months were some of the richest months he would have in his life, with a concentration of friends old and new, and devotions ever more heartfelt.

And that is why I could go off to Amherst with the illusion that I could see him right away after I returned. That was a week ago. But the following day the word came that he was truly in his last hours. Tom McDonough, caring for him, brought me into his bedroom Wednesday morning, and I found Fr. Arne with his face swollen from medication. He was a master of language, but now was straining and frustrated because he was trying to tell me something and couldn't get the words out. I held his hand and began to talk to him, remembering so many of the things we had done together, but most notably his gentle and clever move in drawing me into the Church, and his loving Memorial Mass for my beloved wife, Judy.

His drawing me into the Church became the subject of comic legend. I told the story seven years ago when he had presided over my baptism. It was October 2009—the day of the Red Mass in Washington held to mark the opening of the courts of justice. The Supreme Court would open its term the next day, and most of the Justices would be present at St. Matthew's Cathedral.

Following the Mass, my wife and I were on the way to the luncheon, to catch up with the Scalias. We encountered Fr. Arne on the way—a lovely surprise, for I hadn't seen him since I'd met him years earlier at the Opus Dei house in New York. But instead of giving me the "big hello" he offered a friendly chiding: "You," he said, "are the most notable figure standing for so long now at the threshold of the Church—but not coming across. What has been holding you back?"

I was caught off guard, and in mild desperation, I dipped into the Bert Lahr repertoire from *The Wizard of Oz*: "C-c-c-courage," I said, recalling the Cowardly Lion. "That's what put the 'ape' in apricot, and that's what I haven't got."

Whew, I thought: I finessed that one. About a week later I joined a friend, newly arrived, who was attending noon Mass with Fr. Arne. Father wasn't expecting me, which made the next move all the more remarkable. He said in his homily that "the one thing connecting these two readings together today is . . . c-c-c-courage."

All right, I had to concede, the point was made, and it was time to stop wavering. And thinking back to that moment now, I was struck by the quick wit and genius he showed in reaching me that way.

He died Wednesday evening; I had seen him in the morning. I made it back to his room that night to kneel at his bedside, kiss him on his shoulder and cheek, and pray again. His face had changed: no longer swollen, he looked himself, and looked peaceful. He had his familiar smile, which seemed to say that he was glad to see you and eager as ever to hear what you had to tell him. . . .

When Fr. Arne would do talks for us during a retreat, he would begin by saying, "My Lord, I know that you can hear me now." The going hunch is that Father's time in Purgatory will last about a nanosecond, and so some of us will be thinking to ourselves, "Fr. Arne, I know that you can hear me now."

—*Hadley Arkes*
Founder and Director of the James Wilson Center on
National Rights and the American Founding; professor
emeritus at Amherst College. This recollection is abridged
from a column on July 26, 2017, at thecatholicthing.org, as
"What Fr. Arne Shaped"; reprinted with permission.

*   *   *

I first met Fr. Arne when I went to a talk by Fr. Jacques Philippe at the CIC. Within minutes, Fr. Arne had heard about my plans for the next few years, my difficulties over the past few years, and suggested that he might be able to help me out in some professional areas. Even at our first meeting he proved himself to be an example of John Paul II's definition of a priest: "A man for others."

And that impression continued during our few conversations, when personal spiritual direction was interspersed with philosophical commentary and with jokes about our current culture. It seemed to me that the abstract world was eminently practical for him, that philosophy and theology best understood would immediately help us to live our lives more perfectly. This, of course, for Fr. Arne meant living it more closely in union with Jesus Christ.

Fr. Arne—even in the few encounters I had with him—witnessed to me what a fulfilled fatherhood can look like. His heroic suffering and joyful demeanor even to the end are gifts that I will ask for the grace to live up to when it is my time to go.

—*Peter Atkinson, actor*

*   *   *

Senator Jim Buckley once said within earshot of me that the only place we are all really equal is at the altar rail. Fr. Arne's witness to that reality has always been striking. Manning the closest tabernacle to the White House at the Catholic Information Center, he treats everyone the same: beloved by God and therefore by Fr. Arne! I don't remember the first time I realized I was loved by him, because each time I found it powerful. I had done nothing to earn it. . . . And he had a sixth sense about him. He would always gently tease me about what I was doing on my phone. "Praying the Liturgy of the Hours?" I can't remember now when he said or if he said those words. If you were checking Twitter you probably knew what I was up to. And I had just enough of the tinge of defensiveness to know I was blessed by a good father looking out for me. For as long as I'll live I won't forget seeing him at the Becket Fund dinner in New York, in 2017. My understanding had been that he had been in his final hours. He was supposed to be on his death bed, and yet here he had taken the train from DC—something that exhausts me on a good day—and was greeting his brothers and sisters and spiritual children. I'm pretty sure he saw straight to the heart of my soul that night as the pure of heart can, and I saw joy and peace in Christ and believed it real, and the only desire of the heart that matters.

—*Kathryn Jean Lopez, Senior Fellow,*
National Review Institute

* * *

I remember where I was when I learned that Fr. Arne had died: with a family, many of whom knew Fr. Arne personally. We were about to sit down to eat—to ask the Lord to bless our meal and an email came through. Oddly, there was little sadness among the group, but rather, as we gave the Lord thanks for the gift of our food, we also returned thanks for the gift of Fr. Arne's life.

Later that evening, in an email circulated among his friends, I tried to capture the feeling of the moment:

Perhaps it's strange to say this—but I do not feel touched by pain or sadness at this moment. We die as we live—and it would seem that the mark of a good life is a good death. In some measure the whole of life is a preparation for that moment when the soul takes flight in order to make its return back to the house of the Father. The trajectory of Fr. Arne's life and death seems to be a cause for great joy as we recognize God's grace made manifest in such a great priest and friend.

Those words are as true now as they were then.

—*Fr. Justin Huber, priest, Archdiocese of Washington, DC*

* * *

He was my spiritual advisor, and many much better people sought and benefitted from his counsel. (One day I showed up for my monthly consultation . . . and who should waltz out of Fr. Arne's office, but one of my priests from St. Mary's Basilica in Alexandria, VA?) With no visible effort, he turned the CIC into a spiritual, intellectual, and social haven for a ton of folks, many of us in politics and law and related professions—most Catholic, some not; mostly conservatives; many of us converts—who struggled to make sense of their lives.

While Fr. Arne was keenly attuned to political affairs and debates, he never pushed. His riff on the faith had a parsimonious, unsentimental, no-nonsense elegance: that guy on the cross wants desperately to be your friend. That's basically it. Are you ready?

That's hardly an opening line aimed at collecting ammunition for some political agenda. Nor would it help fake-spiritualize a life you want to live in any event. It's bone-rattling stuff—and a very good way to put your life in order, and to keep political concerns and distractions in perspective. That, in any event, is what I hope to have learned, and what I think drew so many of us to Fr. Arne. He kept us grounded, and kept us from going nuts.

Don't glorify the dead, Fr. Arne liked to exhort: the souls in Purgatory need your prayers. Done that, Father; but I probably missed the two or three minutes you spent there. Instead, would you kindly intercede for the many friends who remember you so fondly? *Ora pro nobis.*

> —*Michael Greve, Professor of Law at the Antonin Scalia School of Law, George Mason University*

*   *   *

I first met Fr. Arne in April 1988, at the Hoover Institution reception for then-Secretary of Education Bill Bennett. Bennett had just delivered a powerful defense of "Western Culture" at Stanford University—a freshman Great Books course that had become the target of left-wing student activists and of spineless university administrators. Fr. Arne was the young chaplain of the Menlo Park Opus Dei house, and I was the twenty-year old undergraduate who had invited Bennett to Stanford in the first place.

All of us sensed that the stakes that day extended far beyond freshman education and Stanford. At stake was nothing less than the West itself: What made the West good? Why did the West deserve to be defended? How do the Great Books point at great truths beyond themselves? We soon were engaged in an intense discussion about the merits of the Thomistic arguments for the existence of God—I thought we needed to do better, Fr. Arne countered that few today even understood what Aquinas had really said—and before the evening was out, we had begun what would become a decades-long friendship.

In the years that followed, we would have many long hikes in the Marin headlands and many returns to the great questions of God and man: Was it a contingent or necessary fact of history that Christ died for us? What does this mean for us personally? Was Christ's sacrifice once and for all, or is there a sense in which Christian life also necessarily involves sacrifice today? Fr. Arne's answers were clear and consistent. They were bracing and at the opposite end of the "prosperity gospel" or of the smug self-sufficiency of a "happy and clappy" church. They were not always what I wanted to hear, but this certainly did not make them untrue.

And it must be underscored that Fr. Arne practiced what he preached. He remained faithful until the end. He truly made of his life a sacrifice. One might be tempted to say that the far from perfect Church did not deserve the sacrifice of this holy man. But then one would immediately need to add: If we better followed the example of Fr. Arne's holiness, then we would be well on our way towards overcoming the crisis of the Church—and the crisis of the West.

—*Peter Thiel, co-founder of PayPal*
and Palantir Technologies

Acknowledgments

Two friends who made these pages possible are Tom McDonough, who kindly arranged my visits to Fr. Arne's residence during the months of hospice care; and Susan Arellano, whose literary insights have been invaluable, as ever.

Special thanks to those who contributed their moving recollections of Fr. Arne to the book's Appendix: Hadley Arkes, Peter Atkinson, Arthur Brooks, Michael Greve, Fr. Justin Huber, Fr. Roger Landry, Kathryn Jean Lopez, Peter Thiel, Christopher White, and two others who remain anonymous.

I'm grateful to George Weigel for contributing the Foreword to these pages; to another longtime friend and colleague, Robert Royal, whose Faith and Reason Institute is now my institutional home; and to artist Igor Babailov for the portrait that graces the book's cover.

This book began via friendships forged during the past ten years at the Catholic Information Center (CIC) in Washington, DC. Special thanks to Director Fr. Charles Trullols; COO Mitchell Boersma; staff members John Hebert, Rosemary Eldridge, Kevin Jones, Julie Larkin, and Elizabeth Winston; former members Lance Casimir, John Coe, Emily Duffy, Mary-Elizabeth Gervais, Brett Manero, Sarah Moss, Nico Pedriera, and Lindsay Petruccelli; and CIC Board members present and past, especially Pat Cipollone, Leonard Leo, Gerry Mitchell, Cindy Searcy, and Tom Yannucci.

Final thanks are to my husband Nicholas and to our children Frederick, Catherine, Isabel, and Alexandra for their enduring empathy and insights. Our shared hope that Fr. Arne's legacy would live on has been the *sine qua non* of this book.